# HOLLYWOOD IN THE SIXTIES

## by JOHN BAXTER

**THE INTERNATIONAL FILM GUIDE SERIES**
**THE TANTIVY PRESS, LONDON**
**A. S. BARNES & CO., NEW YORK**

# Acknowledgements

THE AUTHOR particularly wishes to thank Charles Katz, Leigh Brackett, Dennis Hopper, Dustin Hoffman, Roger Corman and the many other film-makers who were so generous with information, as well as Scott McQueen for his assistance in compiling Chapter Ten, Anthony Sloman and Barrie Pattison for reading the manuscript and offering countless suggestions for its improvement, and the staff of the British Film Institute, notably the ladies of its Information Department and Library, for their help during research.

For Graham, Millicent and Margaret Nicholson

COVER
Front: John Wayne in *McLintock!*
(courtesy United Artists)
Back: Mia Farrow and John Cassavetes
in *Rosemary's Baby*
(courtesy Paramount)

FIRST PUBLISHED 1972
*Copyright* © 1972 by John Baxter
Library of Congress Catalogue Card No. 70–181065
SBN 90073020 X
ISBN 0–498–01096–1

Filmset by Keyspools Ltd, Golborne, Lancs.
Printed in Great Britain by C. Tinling & Co. Ltd, London and Prescot

# Contents

# 1. Running Down — Please Pass

IN MAY, 1970, Metro-Goldwyn-Mayer put up for auction the props, costumes and impedimenta collected over forty-five years of film-making. Tarzan's loincloth and Rhett Butler's top hat, weapons, furniture, boats, cars and planes from thousands of M-G-M productions were sold, and despite a poignant appeal from the mayor of Culver City to keep them in the possession of Hollywood's children, even the Ruby Slippers from *The Wizard of Oz* went to a collector, for $15,000. Auctioning props was not itself new — the horror-science fiction TV programme *The Outer Limits* had sold its collection a few years before, and the trade in screen incunabula was a Sixties phenomenon — but that M-G-M, custodian of America's dreams and the studio most adept at distilling the essence of its desires, should irreversibly destroy her heritage seemed a symbolic act more final than any *auto da fe*; with it, Hollywood, mythological capital of the century, ceased to exist.

The auction, imitated quickly by 20th Century-Fox, ended a spring-cleaning of the Hollywood film-making complex that continued throughout the Sixties, a process that by 1970 appeared to have destroyed the studio-based film industry on which the city's fame had been built. But Hollywood's main losses during the Sixties were in the abstract areas of árt and tradition rather than on the industrial level. M-G-M sold off its props, yet most of its stages remained intact and operating, and although many companies chose to sell some of their land for redevelopment, in 1970 the majority of Forties film studios still stood. The popular image of Hollywood as a dismantled dream factory peopled by ghosts disguised a less romantic reality. Much had changed; independent and foreign "runaway" productions replaced studio-instigated films; many great artists had retired or died, and with them the distinctive studio styles they had developed. Unemployment was widespread; feather-bedding and over-staffing in the Fifties made Hollywood the most cloistered of closed shops, with the result that key workers were men of middle-age who had held their positions for many years, jealously refusing to train those who might threaten their security. Hollywood's Sixties recession hit all but the most eminent of these experts, dumping them on a labour market where their skills, too expensive

*Peter Kastner in YOU'RE A BIG BOY NOW*

and too specialised for TV and independent production, were unnegotiable.

But despite major alterations in the ownership of the industry, with conglomerates buying in even when their interest in cinema was minimal, the essential studio structure changed little. Producer/director/script/star "packages," the budget reduced by profit-sharing agreements among their participants, became standard, but in hiring out their facilities Fox or M-G-M still supplied most of the technicians, exercised a degree of control over script, promotion and distribution, and acted with much the same independence as they always had. Laments from film buffs over the acquisition of Paramount by Gulf-Western Oil or United Artists by the Transamerica Corporation obscured the fact that in the Thirties General Electric had owned a controlling interest in Warner Brothers, while New York banks traditionally hold the financial balance of power in all American business, including the cinema. In common with managerial variations in any industry over ten years, those of Hollywood studios from 1960 to 1970 were complex. After the disaster of *Cleopatra*, on which 20th Century-Fox's dwindling resources were squandered in an exercise in old-fashioned studio production (in 1962, the year of its release, Fox lost $39.8 million, after taxes), president Spyros Skouras was replaced by Darryl F. Zanuck. Zanuck later resigned in favour of his son Richard, whom he had installed as production manager, and Richard Zanuck was removed in turn when the company, after a brief revival, lost $47½ million in 1966–67. He then joined Warner Brothers, a studio acquired, then dropped again, by Seven Arts, the TV/management organisation, and one which in 1970 belonged to the Kinney group. Decca Records bought Universal and sold part of it to the Revue TV subsidiary of MCA, whereupon MCA bought both the balance of Decca's Universal holding and then Decca itself. Metro-Goldwyn-Mayer, after poor business in the Sixties, passed in 1969 to hotelier Kirk Kerkorian, with CBS's James Aubrey called in to wield the economy hatchet. Most other companies had equally troubled histories, and the scene was confused by the rise of independents — Commonwealth United, Cinema Centre, Cinerama Corporation — whose policies and viability varied widely.

Although the producers' new power and a reliance on outside talent altered the Hollywood scene, major changes were less internal than in the cinema's relationship to world entertainment. During the Fifties, TV finally supplanted cinema as the universal entertainment medium, and despite loud announcements from Hollywood that "Movies Are Better

Than Ever" studios offered cinema audiences a product little different from that which TV produced in competition. Fifties attempts to defeat TV went on, not with improved films in a style totally different from TV, but in direct opposition to it: Pay-TV, in which exclusive rights to new features were sold to small subscription networks; the production of films specifically for TV, where they were passed off as new cinema features; even the sale of film libraries for telecasting, a disastrous waste of resources. These attempts to beat TV on its own ground failed totally. An acceptance of its reduced share of the market, a readjustment, necessarily painful, in staff and financing, and an exploration of new themes as well as a skilled use of the old, might have recovered for Hollywood some of its lost popularity, but instead the studios, with union encouragement, persisted in their unequal struggle, compounding the errors that led to their downfall. The best answer to TV's dominance which even the most flexible studio could invent was to finance its own series, contributing to the rot that by the mid-Sixties had eclipsed the freshness and vitality of live TV drama, replacing it with Minow's "vast wasteland." Industrially the media were bitter opponents, but as Hollywood turned to B-movies, from which TV had chosen to take its material in the Fifties, and as TV, with ninety-minute shows and an emphasis on colour action stories, moved closer to the traditional cinema feature, it became clear that, artistically, their products were identical.

Inside Hollywood, the water was brackish, the pool smaller and the fish correspondingly more greedy and belligerent. Small fry had long since been eaten, and the sharks ruled. Those with a proven capacity for survival held extraordinary power. The successful star now demanded a say in his scripts, as well as a share of the profits (few took less than $1 million out of a major production), while the writer, traditionally in charge of content, regarded his contribution as sufficiently important to control its form on the screen — a claim the director, normally responsible for this translation, usually conceded, since his interest was increasingly in the financial management formerly handled by producers. In this inflation of roles, only the producer was squeezed out and, while many minor figures in this field found themselves abruptly and incurably unemployed, the more skilful, since their interest had been less in art than finance, slipped comfortably into niches in banking and business.

The newly-powerful creative artists had influence, prestige and, where their films were successful, a more equitable share of the profits, but the people and their attitudes did not change, nor were they, as artists, freer to express themselves. Despite the rise of the independent director/producer and the *auteur* scenarist, probably fewer serious films appeared in the Sixties than in the heyday of the studio, when magnanimous producers with an eye to posterity would finance such films from the guaranteed profits of more routine works. With an all-star package the sole bargaining unit, such intellectual luxury was unthinkable, and not even the most adventurous film-maker would waste his time on a property lacking popular potential. Distinguished dramatists found themselves wasting their new freedom in the fabrication of ornate escapism (Ernest Lehman, author of *North by Northwest*, wrote *The Sound of Music* and wrote and produced *Hello, Dolly!*; Stirling Silliphant scripted *Marlowe* and *In the Heat of the Night*), but few protested against this situation, sweetened as it was by a slice of the gross. An agreed standard of "commercial product" prevailed, little different from that of the Forties, and free-lance directors and writers, in whom the studio philosophy was ingrained, were the last to question it.

A restriction of new product to the area of guaranteed box-office success extinguished those *genres* whose appeal, though constant, had been to a minority audience: the housewife's romance, in which Crawford and Davis had starred; the juvenile and animal film, monopolised during the Sixties by the skilful Disney organisation but otherwise ignored; most notably the "problem" picture that had produced Hollywood's most enduring works. Only that hardy weed, the B-film, thrived — Westerns, gangster dramas, wisecracking comedies — and above it, the huge A-features whose tempting potential profit made them Hollywood's most ruthless destroyers of fortune and reputation — the big show musical and the costume epic. In the past, Hollywood supported an *Intolerance*, a *Gone with the Wind* once in a decade. They were glorious aberrations, as rare and transitory as a comet, and deserving of the same awed respect; but in the Sixties extravaganzas became a standard Hollywood product, the "blockbuster." Producers working in this field were graded according to the budgets with which they had proved themselves competent rather than any talent for self-expression or even making money. A $10 million budget was far more likely to be entrusted to a producer of epics whose $5 million effort had lost a fortune rather than to an artist consistently successful with smaller films, since, with the studios lacking a clear lead from audiences as to what they wanted—here the rating system gave TV an advantage Hollywood lost with its tied chains of theatres — traditional criteria no longer applied. The unsuccessful producer at least knew the mechanics of "getting together" a $5 million film; next time he might be lucky.

Emphasis on size rather than quality gave new importance to production values — photography, set design, costumes — with individual studio departments, usually appointed to a film before either writer or director, demonstrating their ability in the hope of an Oscar nomination, and inflating the feeblest story into two hours of exquisitely mounted rubbish. The credit sequence became an art in itself, spun out to provide an attractive preamble to films seldom living up to this promise. Many attended *A Walk on the Wild Side* (1962) only for Saul Bass's superb titles of a black cat pacing through photogenic slums to Elmer Bernstein's raucous theme, and left before Edward Dmytryk's doomed version of Nelson Algren unfolded. With major scenarists playing the production game, and Hollywood's capacity for original thought blighted by the anti-Red blacklist that stunted many important careers and smothered serious statement for ten years, studios relied on journalists and magazine writers of the sort Warners had recruited in the early Thirties to support its output of B-movies. Vital reservoirs of skill and knowledge drained away as the studios laid off seasoned writers in favour of these cheap imitations. In 1960, when the Screen Writers' Guild went on a six-month strike to stem the tide of dismissals and non-renewals of contract, only forty-eight writers were under contract to Hollywood studios, compared with sixty-seven in 1950 and four-hundred-and-ninety in 1945. An imbalance between polish and content, and the dearth of skilled writers, led to an industry where the threadbare dialogue and high-camp posturing of a Maria Montez romance could, with the expenditure of $40 million and a flood of tasteless bally-hoo, be offered as *Cleopatra*, the greatest film of all time.

No correction of the disparity between cost and content was possible as long as studios pursued their short-sighted recruitment policy. New arrivals, like writers, came from other media where their talent to amuse had been proven at the bank, and a promising TV or stage director without cinema experience was always preferred to an unknown whose ambition was solely to make movies. The system, just as in the early Thirties when stage directors were imported in quantity, offered short-term advantages but collapsed as the newcomers' lack of sympathy with the cinema became evident, and all but the best retreated into routine B-features reminiscent of the work they knew. Although some directors from the stage (Arthur Penn, Mike Nichols) or TV (John Frankenheimer, Sam Peckinpah, Jack

Smight) stayed and endured, the New York orientation of recruitment did not offer the same quantity of talent as slow studio apprenticeship. With the new East Coast emphasis, Hollywood films achieved a glibness and polish more redolent of Manhattan than the Californian hothouse, and discarded studio and backlot for location shooting. As late as 1955, Mitchell Leisen's *Bedevilled* could proudly be billed by M-G-M as "the first film shot on location in France," but Otto Preminger's use of Washington and Michigan respectively for *The Court Martial of Billy Mitchell* (1955) and *Anatomy of a Murder* (1960) finally severed the studio umbilical, and by 1962 30% of Hollywood's major product was shot overseas. Technique too reflected a New York ambiance, with hand-held cameras more in use as American cinematographers capitalised on European engineering and style; 16mm footage blown up to 35mm was increasingly common,

*Super-Panavision: John Frankenheimer (left) with long-lens 70mm. camera on GRAND PRIX*

and unnoticeable. With the skill of Daniels, Shamroy and Garmes by now anachronistic, cinematography passed into the hands of New Yorkers like Haskell Wexler, William Fraker and Laszlo Kovacs, apostles of *cinéma vérité* style, though James Wong Howe, Conrad Hall and Joe MacDonald, pioneers of naturalism in photography, produced the most impressive camerawork of the Sixties, adjusting to the new techniques but integrating them with the best of the old.

With anamorphic processes the norm, the 1.85:1 ratio of so-called "wide screen" universally replaced Academy Frame's 1.33:1, and revivals of standard features suffered a brutal cropping. Cinerama's unequal struggle with three-image presentation ended after *The Wonderful World of the Brothers Grimm* (Henry Levin, George Pal, 1962) and *How the West Was Won* (1962), its first story films. The next exercise in Cinerama narrative, *It's a Mad, Mad, Mad, Mad World* (Stanley Kramer, 1963) used single-lens 65mm given width for Cinerama's wide-screen theatres by an anamorphic lens. The resulting 65mm Cinemascope, known as Ultra-Panavision, was boosted by special lenses and, notwithstanding width without height (the ratio was 2.75:1) and a consequent letter-box effect, suited John Frankenheimer's exciting car-racing romance, *Grand Prix* (1966). Non-anamorphic 70mm, the most satisfying of all formats, offering size without loss of density or sharpness, became standard after its skilled use by Freddie Young in David Lean's *Lawrence of Arabia* (1962) and *Doctor Zhivago* (1966), though the spread of the hard-ticket and road-show philosophies, along with high prices, neutralised its attraction, and by 1970 most units were again shooting in 35mm, reserving 70mm for release prints only. As the Fifties' technical experiments — 3-D, attempts (ToddAO, Vista-Vision) to duplicate the impact of Cinemascope — faded like their entre-preneurs, an energetic few persisted with novelty as a substitute for quality. William Castle, father of "Emergo" and other grotesque gimmicks, offered *Thirteen Ghosts* (1960) in "Illusion-O"; "ghost viewer" glasses with one red and one blue lens allowed sceptics who "didn't believe in ghosts" to look through the blue panel and expunge some double-exposure images of phantoms, while believers peering through the red gelatine could have their faith confirmed. Even if faults in the process had not made the images visible whether with glasses or without, "Illusion-O" would still have been doomed to instant extinction, and its producer returned, perhaps grate-fully, to the thrillers of which he had proved himself in the Forties an expert producer and director; among the results was the eerie *Rosemary's Baby*.

*DOCTOR ZHIVAGO: Julie Christie*

Electronovision, developed for *Harlow* (Alex Segal, 1965) and a feature version of Richard Burton's Broadway *Hamlet* (John Gielgud, 1964), used TV cameras and videotape to bypass studio costs and controlled blurring to erase the lines of the TV image, but with little success and a predictable outcry from the unions. The most unlikely experiment was Smellovision, reviving the process Charles Weiss had marketed as AromaRama. *Scent of Mystery* (Jack Cardiff, 1960) was accompanied by a "programme" of odours fed into the theatre air-conditioning. To nobody's surprise, smells varied in strength and timing from theatre to theatre, or blended with the preceding selection to create some appalling effects. The process, in the words of its backer, Mike Todd Jnr., was "almost instantaneously rejected by the public," and *Scent of Mystery*, retitled *Holiday in Spain*, finally went out *sans* smells to unsuccessful general release.

Although the cinema revolution of the Fifties rocked Hollywood, precipitating long-overdue readjustments, the ebb of the New Wave left world cinema, and Hollywood, diminished but essentially unchanged. Louis de Funès and Bourvil remained France's top box-office attractions even when Godard reigned, just as a vogue for French, Czech or even American *nouvelle vague* films left undimmed the admiration of all nations for the white-bread charm of Rock Hudson and Doris Day. With TV audiences demonstrating that old subjects, styles and stars retained their appeal, Hollywood would willingly have starred the same names in appropriate vehicles until Doomsday, had not time intervened. Age took its toll of the established stars, and a decade of conservatism and parsimony in recruitment left nobody to replace them. The survivors' mask-like faces showed that make-up and plastic surgery contributed as much to many performances as acting. Gary Cooper had taken to hiding his baldness by playing roles (e.g. *Garden of Evil*, 1954, *Man of the West*, 1958) without once, even when asleep, removing his hat, and actors like Lee J. Cobb offered directors a choice of toupees. Without new stars of authority to replace them, John Wayne and James Stewart soldiered on in romantic roles well past the age when others had accepted unclehood and the wheelchair. The necrology of Hollywood in the Sixties is appallingly long. Among actors, active and retired, who died, were Spencer Tracy, Gary Cooper, Alan Ladd, Peter Lorre, Harpo and Chico Marx (as well as their foil Margaret Dumont), Nelson Eddy and Jeanette MacDonald, Stan Laurel, Mae Murray, Linda Darnell, Judy Holliday, Clara Bow, Dick Powell, Marilyn Monroe, Clark Gable, Boris Karloff, Judy Garland, Buster Keaton, Charles Laughton; among directors, producers and technicians, David Selznick, Michael Curtiz, Jerry Wald, Frank Borzage, Anthony Mann, Robert Rossen, Leo McCarey, Josef von Sternberg, William Daniels, Karl Freund, Alfred Newman, Ben Hecht and countless others. Even the appearance of Steve McQueen, Robert Redford, William Fraker and Jack Smight is at best a consolation prize.

In the shift to a B-film mentality, a whole generation of Hollywood actors and actresses disappeared. While stalwarts like Bette Davis and Joan Crawford exercised the shreds of their drawing power in chillers and horror films, the personalities who would have replaced them — Anne Baxter, Dorothy Malone, Dorothy McGuire, Joanne Woodward, Grace Kelly — as well as the *jeunes premiers* with whom they should have been matched — Richard Egan, Cliff Robertson, Robert Stack — retreated, bereft of suitable roles, into TV. The Sixties stars, predictably, are B-movie talents who graduated, like the films in which they had always appeared, to disconcerting eminence. Often able, they nevertheless carry with them the connotations earned in the programme picture, and personae that type-casting has made indelible: hard blondes Kim Novak and Carroll Baker, heavies Lee Marvin and Anthony Quinn, teasers Ann-Margret and Lee Remick, scatter-brains Marilyn Monroe and Shirley MacLaine, and Rock Hudson, the Robert Cummings of the Atomic Age. After the actors' strike of 1960, which won rises in minimum pay between 11% and 81%, the days of the cheap talent-school starlet who sweated to stardom under a seven-year contract had gone forever. Far better, most studios reasoned, to exploit the trained graduates of low-budget movies, especially since slightly more lavish versions of such films seemed to satisfy the public, and young actors of talent trained in the Hollywood school were abruptly out of date — Michael Parks, Mariette Hartley, Jim Hutton, Diane Varsi, and Yvette Mimieux among them. Only the persistent growth in skill and authority of Robert Redford, Lola Albright, Peter Falk, Donald Sutherland, Tuesday Weld and Paul Newman offers much hope of an authentic American stardom of the Seventies, and even in their cases one doubts the ability of Hollywood to provide them with appropriate material; more and more, such artists must turn to European films or productions by independent American directors. Perhaps in selling its props and disposing of its land, Hollywood destroyed something more subtle than mere extraneous holdings — the soul of American cinema.

*A MAN FOR ALL SEASONS: Paul Scofield as Thomas More faces his inquisitors*

# 2. The Death of Kings

IN THE general inflation of B-film subjects and talents, the "idea" picture and prestige artist sank of their own weight. Myths and archetypal figures, on which the B-film based its appeal — cowboys, private eyes, show business personalities — had been of little concern to serious Hollywood film-makers, whose interest lay wholly in ideas, a preoccupation that robbed them of an audience in the mindless Sixties. Most of the Fifties masters, inheritors of Goldwyn's pretensions and Selznick's "tradition of quality," gasped for financial air in a Hollywood obsessed by profit, interested only in the cheap sure-fire success or the promise of immense profit from a "block-buster." As less energetic talents faded, a few hardy individuals thrived. Fred Zinnemann, following the success of *The Sundowners* (1960), where attractive Australian locations disguised an amiable Down-Under Western, surprised audiences with *Behold a Pale Horse* (1964), a harsh and commercially disastrous story of political friction in Spain, with Gregory Peck an obstinate terrorist and Anthony Quinn his antagonist. Following that, he then achieved profit and Oscars with a scrupulous if stage-bound adaptation of Robert Bolt's *A Man For All Seasons* (1966), Paul Scofield playing a suitably humane Sir Thomas More. After declining from the heights of *The Best Years of Our Lives* to *Ben Hur*,

the career of William Wyler seemed ended with *The Children's Hour* (1962), a belated but routine film of Lillian Hellman's lesbian drama, his excellent earlier version of which (*These Three*, 1936) had lacked, by Hays Office edict, any mention of sexual deviation. A brief return to critical approval with *The Collector* (1965), from John Fowles's sinister novel of a disturbed young man (Terence Stamp) who "collects" a beautiful girl (Samantha Eggar) as one acquires a butterfly, was not capitalised on with *How to Steal a Million* (1966), a romantic comedy-adventure in the *Charade* style (but showing the need of a Peter Stone script) with an attractive Audrey Hepburn and Peter O'Toole, the latter replacing George C. Scott, fired by Wyler on the first day of shooting for indiscipline. Nor did *Funny Girl* (see Chapter Four) offer much recompense, marking, even though some skill was shown in the enlivening of empty plot and performances, the nadir of Wyler's creativity.

Idea films that in the Fifties might have intrigued audiences fell glumly flat a decade later. Stanley Kramer, acknowledged dean of the "problem picture," directed some stiff dramas, shot with a technical perfection by then outdated. It is a paradox of Kramer's Sixties career that the features on which he acted as producer are more genuinely aware of Sixties problems and infinitely better made than anything he offered as director: Richard Wilson's thoughtful Western *Invitation to a Gunfighter* (1964) with Yul Brynner as a suave gunman whose name, Jules Gaspard D'Estaing should, he explains to his baffled employers, be pronounced "with just a *touch* of dipthong"; *A Child Is Waiting* (1963), in which John Cassavetes directed Judy Garland in a rare and touching role as a teacher of subnormal children; and *Pressure Point* (1962), a version by Hollywood renegade Hubert Cornfield of a section from Robert Lindner's "The Jet-Propelled Couch," in which neo-Nazi Bobby Darin is saved from insanity, via some surrealistic dream sequences, by psychiatrist Sidney Poitier. *Inherit The Wind* (1960) was a version of the Scopes "Monkey Trial" with Spencer Tracy as Clarence Darrow, Fredric March as William Jennings Bryan and Gene Kelly as H. L. Mencken, all disguised under libel-proof aliases, and although Kramer convincingly recreated a small town occupied by hordes of visitors anxious to see evolution put on trial (at one point, Kelly describes it as "the buckle on the Bible belt"), a false romance between the defendant (Dick York) and a fundamentalist minister's daughter strained credibility, despite Claude Akins's vigorously ranting demagogue, a hypnotic performance. *Judgment at Nuremberg* (1961), Abby Mann's attempt to

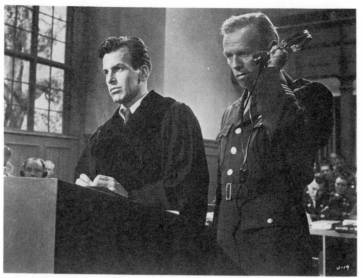

*JUDGMENT AT NUREMBURG: Maximilian Schell, Richard Widmark*

humanise the Nuremberg war crime trials, and *Ship of Fools* (1965), from Katherine Anne Porter's gloomy novel of symbolic high-jinks on a Thirties ocean liner, adopted the venerable *Grand Hotel* formula so useful in pre-war Hollywood, adding in both cases the fashionable dressing of safe attacks on anti-Semitism and Fascism. Similar caution marked *Guess Who's Coming to Dinner?* (1968), an assault on racial intolerance whose success stemmed from a tacit endorsement of middle-class values. Complacent parents Katharine Hepburn and Spencer Tracy, initially appalled by the intention of their daughter to marry a Negro, relent when her choice is revealed as wealthy Nobel Prize-winning doctor Sidney Poitier, a catch so impressive that one senses it would not have mattered if he had been a midget as well. Among Kramer's Sixties films, *It's a Mad, Mad, Mad, Mad World* (1963), a lurid and suggestive anthology of every pratfall gag from the history of Hollywood B-comedy, remains the most vividly memorable. Why he essayed this extraordinary work, whose only antecedent is *Hellza-*

19

*THE CARDINAL: Tom Tryon and John Huston*

*poppin!*, will forever remain a mystery but its total consistency to a mindless premise makes delightful cinema.

Always hovering between the pretension of Kramer and the Forties thriller style whose masters he outlasted, Otto Preminger had little cause to thank the Sixties. After a deserved success with *Anatomy of a Murder* (1960), old fashioned court-room drama dressed up with fashionable sex in the person of Lee Remick's teaser rape victim, a search for whose missing briefs occupies defending attorney James Stewart for much of the film, Preminger loosed some arresting near-misses. *Exodus* (1960), an attempt to concentrate the story of Israel and Jewish independence into two hours and one love affair between Paul Newman and Eva Marie Saint, was doomed to

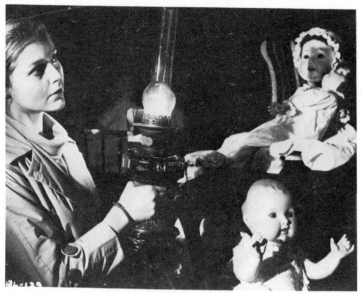

*BUNNY LAKE IS MISSING: Carol Lynley*

failure through its ambition; and in Allen Drury's *Advise and Consent* (1962) only forceful performances from veterans Charles Laughton, as an obese Southern senator, mountainous in crumpled white linen, Gene Tierney as a mask-faced Washington hostess and Franchot Tone as the ailing president, sustained a flat conception of power politics. *The Cardinal* (1963), in trying to do for the Catholic church what *Exodus* did for Judaism, merely offered a religious version of *The FBI Story*; instead of James Stewart assisting in the solution of crimes from 1914 land-grabbing to the arrest of atomic spies, Tom Tryon suffered every test of faith that vexed Catholics of the last century, from birth control to a failure to intervene in Nazi war crimes. Again, a few performances, particularly Romy Schneider as Tryon's prospective lover and John Huston as a crusty Boston Cardinal, held the interest. *In Harm's Way* (1965), an oddly intimate drama of personal relationships against the background of Pearl Harbour, and *Hurry*

21

*Sundown* (1967), where Southern sharecroppers are driven off their land by big business, failed through their indecision, and only *Bunny Lake is Missing* (1965), shot in England with a remarkable cast including Noël Coward as a camp landlord who collects shrunken heads and Laurence Olivier as a policeman investigating the kidnap of Carol Lynley's young daughter, recalled the mastery of *Laura*.

Elia Kazan, more respected than most in the Fifties for his socialist/humanist parables, seems sadly out of place, his subjects as redolent as Kramer's of the Thirties and a time when politics had sufficient glamour to be a successful cinema subject. *Wild River* (1960), with Montgomery Clift as a TVA trouble-shooter easing Jo Van Fleet and her brood off a Mississippi island they have occupied for generations, belongs, despite its gloomily accurate recreation of the Thirties, to an optimistic period when Americans stood more unified on political issues. Also set in a less complex period than the present, *Splendor in the Grass* (1961), although a William Inge film with all that this playwright's style suggests — extravagant romance and dialogue of high-flown folksiness — counterbalances his excesses with a sure eye for character, particularly Pat Hingle as the father, and a genuinely original view of sexual conflict and neurosis from Natalie Wood, even if her fevered performance does seem to suggest that a lack of sex will drive one insane. Following a decline in critical success, Kazan turned wholly to the past, exploring his own heritage as novelist and film-maker. *America, America* (1964) (also known as *The Anatolian Smile*) described with touching and intricate detail his grand-father's adventures in search of an idealised America far from the oppression of his Balkan homeland, a theme he followed in *The Arrangement* (1970), where a successful advertising executive (Kirk Douglas), facing the problems Kazan, in his accurate description of them, shows he himself shared, destroys a meaningless life in search of a purity his ancestors knew, and rebuilds a new existence with the help of an independent and unique woman (Faye Dunaway). More convincing in novel form, Kazan's film of *The Arrangement* captures the Sixties' accidie, but it is *America, America*, with its bleak but hopeful picture of a migrant's dream and the reality he finds, that will survive.

A few directors, perhaps because their ambitions were less inflated than those of Kramer and Kazan, achieved films in which serious ideas had impressive expression. Richard Brooks, a skilled scenarist bogged down for years in stolid melodrama, followed his aggressive *Elmer Gantry*

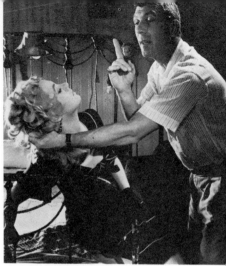

*left: IN COLD BLOOD: Scott Wilson*
*right: ELMER GANTRY: Richard Brooks directs Shirley Jones*

(1960) (in which Burt Lancaster played Sinclair Lewis's ruthless revivalist with authoritative support from Jean Simmons as a pure evangelist and Shirley Jones as the wronged prostitute who destroys him) with the stiffly artificial *Sweet Bird of Youth* (1962), saved by Tennessee Williams's acrid dialogue and a performance of shrewd sensuality and corruption from Geraldine Page as the drunken star to whom Paul Newman's gigolo attaches himself. After the failure of *Lord Jim* (1965), whose lush Eastern colour smothered Joseph Conrad's stiff morality, and the lively though undemanding *The Professionals* (see Chapter Eight), Brooks rallied with *In Cold Blood* (1968). All his films suggest an unextinguished social conscience, a moral rigour struggling for expression, but it is *In Cold Blood* alone, with its documentary harshness, crisp winter photography (again by the remarkable Conrad Hall) and tight performances from Robert Blake and Scott Wilson as the mass-murderers of Truman Capote's non-fiction novel, that shows a Brooks one remembers from *The Blackboard Jungle*.

Robert Rossen, another scenarist of the Forties and doomed, one would

*LILITH*: Warren Beatty, Jean Seberg

have thought, to Brooks's death by profitability, rose above disasters like *Mambo* (1955) and their effete romanticism to create in *The Hustler* (1961) an entertaining and energetic work. Not the masterpiece it was hailed to be — Rossen inherited too much of Hollywood to make a film in which the professionally skilled hero is not also an Adonis, the evil mastermind does not wear black and talk glibly of morality and "character," and the essential conflict (here the contrast in temperament between top pool players "Fast Eddie" and "Minnesota Fats") is not symbolised by an exciting action sequence — *The Hustler* stands out in a period of near-misses for its accurate technique and perception. Rossen's control, if slipping in the use of Piper Laurie as a maudlin, drunken and crippled girl friend, never falters with either Paul Newman, Murray Hamilton's effete Southern dilettante or Jackie Gleason's "Fats," a role so precisely appropriate to this actor that one imagines no other in it. His rhetorical "D'ya think this boy's a hustler?" to the assembled onlookers, like the pool-room manager's response when newcomer Newman asks if the big-time pool room has a bar ("No bar, no pin-ball machine. Just pool. This here is *Ames*, son"), has the authentic tone of patient condescension, the feel of professional aristocracy which a few individuals share in every human endeavour. By contrast, *Lilith* (1964) uses a tranquil, dream-like setting for its love story, the calm of male nurse Warren Beatty's obsession with beautiful mental patient Jean Seberg underlaid with a sense of silent conflicts, of unexpressed evil. Daunting in its complex script and behavioural subtleties, *Lilith* failed commercially, but its intricacy makes one regret even more the premature death in 1966 of this accomplished director.

In a different style, Vincente Minnelli, doyen of M-G-M musicals in the Fifties, achieved a change of emphasis as sweeping as Rossen's to become an assured director of melodrama. Aside from two comedies, *The Courtship of Eddie's Father* (1963), briefly memorable for a sub-plot romance between disc jockey Jerry Van Dyke and his drumming blonde girl-friend Stella Stevens, and the totally unremarkable *Goodbye Charlie* (1964), Minnelli's Sixties films show an almost Twenties skill with elaborate emotions. *Home from the Hill* (1960) used Robert Mitchum's rugged force in the role of a Southern rake, disappointed by the effeminacy of his boy (George Hamilton) but finding an echo of his own virility in an illegitimate son (George Peppard). With crisp efficiency, Minnelli re-creates the dissent and gossip of a modern rural town, and shows a flair for action in a pig-hunt sequence whose hair-raising realism is accentuated by an introduction to the pleasures of this bloody sport delivered by Mitchum with a sportsman's relish. Neither his remake of the Valentino vehicle *The Four Horsemen of the Apocalypse* (1962), at least as slow but far less atmospheric than Rex Ingram's 1921 version, nor the overheated romance of *The Sandpiper* (1965), little more than an excuse for Elizabeth Taylor and Richard Burton to demonstrate their obvious physical passion against attractive Big Sur locations, show Minnelli at full stretch, but *Two Weeks in Another Town* (1962), not wholly because of its resonances with his earlier masterpiece *The Bad and the Beautiful*, remains one of the decade's most impressive films. With Kirk Douglas extending his role as brutal but talented film-maker of the earlier drama, Minnelli shows him as an actor without future or friends, lured from the peace of a sanitorium by an offer of work on a film being produced by old associate Edward G. Robinson in Rome. The offer is as spurious as the friendship, an attempt by Robinson to save his failing career by exploiting Douglas's talent, but out of the agony comes a new confidence and the first true understanding by Douglas of his nature. Minnelli's skill in design gives the Roman setting a haunting life; an ornate

*THE SANDPIPER: Elizabeth Taylor*

fountain, glimpsed by Douglas after the revelation that his corrupt ex-wife (Cyd Charisse) gave herself even to the obese Robinson, becomes a writhing stew of lasciviously entwined limbs, while a party scene at Charisse's villa, with Eighteenth century sphinxes supporting a crooning Negress and satin hangings spilling down the walls, silkily evokes high society decadence.

In their persistent rejection of B-film plots and style, a natural affinity for big subjects and budgets, and, on the debit side, an acceptance of the enfeebled moral conscience which for decades had passed in Hollywood for insight, a few Fifties recruits to Hollywood placed themselves alongside older directors like Kazan and Zinnemann. Blake Edwards, Ralph Nelson, Norman Jewison and Elliot Silverstein represent the more commercially successful of these, but among those who balance pretension with a clearer apprehension of modern morality and attitudes, John Frankenheimer and Robert Mulligan excel.

26

*THE FIXER: Alan Bates*

Essentially a master of the technological drama, expert in its clashing visuals and integration of background into action, Frankenheimer's films in this style are discussed in Chapter Ten. Even his simpler productions reflect a love and understanding of machinery: roaring racing cars in *Grand Prix* (1966), where mechanical rules apply equally to the race and the love affairs through which it threads, and in *The Train* (1965) both the locomotive itself, used to carry French art treasures out of Paris as the booty of a cultivated German general (Paul Scofield), and the plot engineered by resistance fighter Burt Lancaster to route the consignment back to its original destination. *The Young Savages* (1961), describing Lancaster's investigation of juvenile delinquency in New York, and *All Fall Down* (1962), which analyses the decay of a young man's admiration for his older brother, concern themselves with the mechanics of relationships, and even when betraying themselves with simplistic morality and a casually romantic style reminiscent of the Fifties, contrive to involve us in the *way* Karl Malden and Angela Lansbury in *All Fall Down* neglect their younger son (Brandon de Wilde) and idolise the older (Warren Beatty), in the mechanism of his seduction of Eva Marie Saint, in the chemistry of his sexual attraction to all who meet him. *Birdman of Alcatraz* (1962), inherited, like *The Train*, from another director when script and circumstances proved too much (*The Train* was begun by Arthur Penn, who filmed for only four days; *Birdman* by Charles Crichton), oppressively but skilfully captures the rebirth of a man, showing in intimate detail his evolution from a vegetating brute to thinking being as the birds who inhabit his solitary confinement cell become an object of study and love. In its use of light and shade to convey subtleties for which no other means exist, *Birdman of Alcatraz* sustains its length more than *The Fixer* (1968), Frankenheimer's version of Bernard Malamud's novel of anti-Semitic pogroms in Nineteenth century Russia, but it is perhaps understandable that Frankenheimer prefers the later and, superficially, more profound film. The scene of Alan Bates refusing amnesty from David Warner's prison official and demanding the exoneration of a trial is, he feels, the best of his work, a view with which his admirers may not agree.

Robert Mulligan's talent, less substantial than Frankenheimer's, thrives on familiar traditions: family, romance, boy-meets-girl, local-boy-makes-good. His best film, *To Kill a Mockingbird* (1963) recalls Clarence Brown in its noble small-town lawyer, played by Gregory Peck, an expert in such parts, its story of a Negro defended against an unjust rape charge, and in the accuracy of its insight into Peck's relationship with his children and their reaction to this and other events in their life one summer in 1932. Sanitising Gavin Lambert's novel, *Inside Daisy Clover* (1966) became a story of Natalie Wood's rise from wandering beach-bum child to Hollywood star more reminiscent of a studio biography than the examination and criticism of American myths Lambert so skilfully drew, though Ruth Gordon's eccentric portrait of Daisy's mother, "The Dealer," transferred intact. Steve McQueen, afforded more opportunities than most directors by Mulligan, gave coherent voices to the heroes of *Baby the Rain Must Fall* (1965) and *Love with the Proper Stranger* (1964); his feckless wandering Southerner in the first, with songs disguising the aimlessness of his life and the pain he causes his disoriented wife (Lee Remick), and flip jazz musician of the second, nervously involved with a girl (Natalie Wood) whom he has made pregnant, show collaboration of the highest order between director and star. Mulligan raises the second of these films to the level of a minor classic with his realistic picture of the city's dustier corners:

*INSIDE DAISY CLOVER: Natalie Wood*

the cluttered apartment of Edie Adams, McQueen's wisecracking stripper girl friend, a delightful cameo; the deafening clamour of a union hiring hall where the film opens; empty Sunday streets and the seedy mechanics of the abortionist's trade, carried out in a carpetless, unfurnished apartment in a silent building. Mulligan seldom struck this balance of realism and insight in his remaining Sixties films, least of all in *Up the Down Staircase* (1967), an invitation to histrionics gleefully accepted by Sandy Dennis, and a routine Western, *The Stalking Moon* (1969), with Gregory Peck again upholding familial virtue, this time in a frontier setting. Even in his best films, as in the later Frankenheimer, one senses the soft centre, an urge to romanticise which, however vital to the mixture of flair and sentiment we now recognise as the unique flavour of the Forties, sets a director out of phase with the Sixties, a decade impatient of style, if lamentably lacking in an alternative.

# 3. Easterners

A CONCEPT of "the coast" dominated Hollywood from the Twenties when, physically, intellectually and industrially remote from traditional centres of art and business, Hollywood became an embassy to the outside world, manufacturing products whose artificiality could be excused as expressions of an idealised truth about America. The destruction of this shop-window atmosphere in the Fifties, and with it the philosophy that Hollywood had a duty to explain America to the world, when reinforced by the non-appearance of the war that had twice intervened to destroy Hollywood's traditional enemy, the cinema of Europe, ruptured the dome of professional expertise by which it had justified its excesses and barred the unruly. Although the failure of the Fifties was primarily industrial, Hollywood's courage had also been severely shaken, and traditional in-

*Independent: Frank Perry directs Burt Lancaster in THE SWIMMER*

cursions into the movie colony by independent talents met not the usual wall of resistance that, when penetrated, revealed a trap into which even the most skilful fell, but a nervous and unresisting confusion. As foreign films bypassed conventional distribution chains to snatch the large and un-noticed intellectual and student audience, the growing vitality of East Coast art, particularly on Broadway, gave to New York writers and pro-ducers a new power. Inventive Easterners like John Frankenheimer and Arthur Penn who had produced Hollywood features in the Fifties, only to recoil from the philistine studio establishment, returned with greater autonomy, scouts for what was to be a successful invasion.

Attitudes varied to the fall of Hollywood's defences. Some directors, like Frank Perry and Joseph Strick, were sufficiently established outside to ignore it. Others chose to divide their time, producing films both in Holly-wood and New York, though generally with studio money, while another larger group, men like Franklin J. Schaffner, Norman Jewison, Ralph

*MICKEY ONE: Arthur Penn with Ghislain Cloquet on camera*

*THE MIRACLE WORKER: Anne Bancroft and Patty Duke*

Nelson, David Swift and Blake Edwards, whose slick, commercial style showed that they had long been Hollywood people *in petto*, plunged grate-fully into the West Coast pool. Perhaps the greatest impact was made by a few stage and TV directors who remained, emotionally and artistically, grounded in New York: Arthur Penn, Sidney Lumet and Mike Nichols. All three coincided in a common sensibility (and religion), a turning-away from some myths and the embrace of others, often no less venerable but chosen with the new America in mind. Impatient with the simplistic socio-logy which had sustained serious Hollywood cinema since the war, they turned to an examination of personal problems and those of intimate groups as a means of analysing the temper of the time. Rather than giants of the community, they chose to study, and occasionally glorify, the out-cast and the loner whose confusion and alienation seemed closely related to that of American society.

Arthur Penn's films represent a perfect synthesis of Hollywood technique and that psychological precision the best of Broadway drama conveys. On the basis of his direction of two successful William Gibson plays, *Two for the See-Saw* and *The Miracle Worker*, he persuaded Hollywood of his ability, and undismayed by the painful experiment of *The Left-Handed Gun* (1958) tackled West Coast studios once more in 1962 with *The Miracle Worker*, which, though shot in the East, was backed by Hollywood. Anne Bancroft, whom Penn had discovered for *Two for the See-Saw* and directed on Broadway in both plays, starred as the woman who teaches the young deaf-mute Helen Keller (Patty Duke) to speak. Reflecting the mistaken naturalism of the play's original staging (Robert Wise in his 1962 film of *Two for the See-Saw* more accurately mirrors Gibson's sparse style, which Penn admits he missed in both the stage and film versions of *The Miracle Worker*), the film is saved by Anne Bancroft's dazzling performance, and the casually effective East Coast rural settings, a foretaste of Penn's sensitivity for American landscape. *Mickey One* (1965), shot in Chicago with a script which, though Columbia had never read it, had the implied endorsement of *The Miracle Worker*'s success, remains Penn's most provocative and difficult film, a flight through the urban wilderness by night-club comic Mickey (Warren Beatty) who, chased by a phantom gang partly of his own imagining, hides among the drop-outs and junk-heaps, sustained by a cringing agent (Teddy Hart) and a ravaged club owner (Franchot Tone), his only friend. Penn regrets the obscurity of the story, with its ambiguous encounters between Mickey and a lackadaisical girl (Alexandra Stewart), Kafkaesque settings and odd climax of an enormous self-destroying sculpture (called *Yes*) going wild in a courtyard as art dilettantes look on (the scene drew a real fire brigade, which smothered the work in unscripted foam), and would like to remake it with a simpler narrative, but inky photography (Ghislain Cloquet) and Eddie Sauter's swooping jazz score (with Stan Getz solos) gives *Mickey One* a unique character worth preserving.

Theatre continued to underly Penn's career. After the unhappy experience of *The Train*, he tackled Horton Foote's novel and play *The Chase*, a long-time project. Backed by Sam Spiegel (who, disliking Penn's final cut, later had it re-edited in England and a John Barry score added), Penn commissioned a script by Lillian Hellman, whose *Toys in the Attic* he had directed on Broadway. In four years of preparation, *The Chase* (1966) evolved into a dissection of the climate of violence oppressing America.

Penn intended no specific reference to the Kennedy assassination in his incident of a prisoner senselessly murdered (thus bringing to an arbitrary end some complex relationships), but the film's release so close to the event shows his remarkable sensitivity to developing legends. Precisely evocative of small-town tensions and the roots of social disquiet, *The Chase* is let down by James Fox's weak son of E. G. Marshall's Southern tycoon, but Robert Redford, as the town scapegoat returning to twist the conscience of Fox and Jane Fonda (lovers even though Fonda is married to Redford), and Marlon Brando as the honest sheriff whose devotion to duty brings him brutal beatings and final physical, though not moral, defeat, both produce powerful playing. Visually, the film reflects the long hot summer when boredom abrades the nerves, stirring the lazy town into sexual acquisitiveness and senseless violence. As the bored middle-class flourish their guns and feel each other up at drunken parties, Redford flees through the swamps into a sunset, foreshadowing his capture in a junk-yard alight with burning tyres rolled into the wrecks by sadistic onlookers — a scene giving grim substance to the film's intimations of social disquiet.

From this reappearance in a new and dangerous form of the frontier concept of society as a balance of personal power based on the calculated use of force (one exploited more directly in the school of bloody thrillers Don Siegel began), Penn in *Bonnie and Clyde* (1967) created a key film. Again precisely reflecting American myths, it elevated sleazy Thirties killers Bonnie Parker and Clyde Barrow to national heroes, focuses for the hopes of a generation to whom classic virtues were absurdly anachronistic. Unable to find anything worthy of emulation in a society devoid of social purpose, young audiences saw Penn's couple as saints for a disenchanted age: the bored but sensitive small-town girl who achieves national fame, and the minor thug, unimaginative and impotent, who conquers his inadequacies with a beautiful girl and dies with her in a fabulous martyrdom. Evoking the flat Mid-Western landscape with his usual skill, Penn subtly combines fantasy with a sense of America's impassive beauty, showing the bandits as sailors in a desert of wheat, forest and water. Declining to imitate the Thirties too closely, he selects elements recalling their glamour — "We're In the Money" from *Golddiggers of 1933*, Charles Henderson's and Rudy Vallee's "Deep Night" crooned by the latter in an authentic arrangement under the credits while pictures of the real Bonnie and Clyde pass by

*THE CHASE: Marlon Brando, Janice Rule*

*BONNIE AND CLYDE: Faye Dunaway, Warren Beatty*

to the precise click of a Box Brownie. As Gordon Gow noted (and Penn agreed), the film discards the real couple for "Bonnie and Clyde as they would have liked to look," and abandons truth for the myth with which envious contemporaries surrounded them.

After the impact of *Bonnie and Clyde, Alice's Restaurant* (1970), elegaic and calm, seemed an anti-climax, though its theme gave eloquent expression to the problems at which earlier films had merely hinted. Unlike *Mickey One, Alice's Restaurant* had a superficially amusing story whose humour partially disguised the harsh lesson beneath, the tale of Arlo Guthrie's prosecution by rural police for dumping rubbish and his subsequent rejection for military service blending satire on American authority with a critical review of the myths *Bonnie and Clyde* so elegantly glamourised. Independence has, he suggests, a darker side for the person without a sustaining belief and purpose. Arlo, following in the footsteps of his legendary father Woody, makes his own way, rejecting, often harshly, those invitations to pleasure — sex with an old comrade of his father, the wife of a drop-out friend, or with a brainless "collector" of pop stars ("I've made it with the drummer of the Democratic Convention. . . . You might be an album one day") — that his stoic morality cannot countenance. The unsuccessful search by the drop-out generation for a philosophy coalesces in the winter funeral of a young addict, a snow-shrouded rite where folk ballads offer little comfort to the alienated, isolated mourners, and in the nervous tolerance of the small town where Ray and Alice hold open house in a deconsecrated church. (Although the story is true, one cannot help seeing Penn's choice as influenced by this useful symbol of new ideas coffined in the shell of the old.) At the centre of this confusion, through which Arlo moves with the moonstruck solemnity of a true ascetic, even those closest to the new ethic are ill at ease. Penn's final shot shows Alice silent among the trees, the camera zooming in and tracking back simultaneously to show subtle changes in perspective but none in actual proportions, a delicate device suggesting that the universal problems of man are not solved with a mere variation in ritual. "No matter what the sense of motion might be," Penn has said of this image, "the final condition is one of paralysis."

A similar use of style to suggest subliminally the malaise of the Sixties and its sceptical *élite* marks the work of Mike Nichols, most mercurial of the new East Coast talents. Satirist (with Elaine May) and writer, but primarily Broadway producer/director, Nichols started strongly with *Who's Afraid of Virginia Woolf?* (1966), using Edward Albee's scarifying four-cornered dialogue between campus couples as a vehicle for the explosive and commercial Elizabeth Taylor and Richard Burton. Closely related to the stage version, even in the few irrelevant exterior interludes, the film, like Penn's *The Miracle Worker*, mistakenly followed a naturalistic style that clashed with Albee's subtler effects, but Nichols's *début* was auspicious. He followed it with a production among the most successful of the Sixties. Few producers saw any potential in Charles Webb's novel *The Graduate*; money was hard to find, and even the eventual star, minor Broadway actor Dustin Hoffman, disliked both the novel and the prospect of entering big-league film-making. (After making what he felt to be an unsuccessful test, he went back on the dole.) But eventually *The Graduate* (1967) gave Hollywood its

*THE GRADUATE: Dustin Hoffman, Katharine Ross, Anne Bancroft*

long-awaited breakthrough into the elusive 18–25 market, against which so many films and fortunes had been smashed. Even in retrospect, the elements in the film's alchemy do not readily resolve themselves, and though Hoffman's doggy desperation as the intellectual but inexperienced hero touched a responsive chord in the hearts of countless similar young men on college campuses all over the world, *The Graduate*'s essential appeal is as escapism. A sense of the flesh, particularly in the scenes of Hoffman drifting on an air mattress in the family pool, intercut with his afternoon couplings with the bored Mrs. Robinson (Anne Bancroft), conveys real intimacy, but Nichols's satire on the tyranny of social and sexual customs, played for laughs with Hoffman mismanaging even the few responsibilities of his seduction by Mrs. Robinson, has only minimal impact. Like Penn, he recognises that an aspect of wish-fulfilment is essential to any film's success in a society anxious for new myths to replace the old, and makes Hoffman the failure who finally, against all hope, succeeds, his genuine anguish at the wedding of the girl he loves (Katharine Ross) retrieving her even from beyond marriage. No such shrewd manipulation of the audience marked *Catch-22* (1970), in which little of Joseph Heller's surreal humour survived. Although Alan Arkin, as dumbfounded as Dustin Hoffman, but with more technical skill, tries hard as Yossarian, the pilot hero trapped in the web of military illogic, and occasionally Nichols's Spanish locations, dusty and sun-struck, reflect war's lassitude and unreality, *Catch-22*'s lack is one of vitality, of a visual dimension suggesting the book's dramatic, often poignant undercurrent to which Nichols in a long Roman sequence of Felliniesque fantasy gives incorrect emphasis.

Whereas Penn and Nichols reflected the stage in their films and others from TV embraced cinema technique, a few graduates, mainly from the exciting school of live TV drama, used feature films as extensions of the more familiar medium: Franklin Schaffner's *The Best Man* (1964), a thoughtful account of the cool politicking behind a frenzied nomination congress; cameraman Haskell Wexler's directorial *début*, *Medium Cool* (1969), which used TV style for a semi-documentary account of the disorder surrounding another political convention; and more recent works like Michael Ritchie's *Downhill Racer* (1969), where the technique of sports TV serves to tell the story of Robert Redford's ambitious championship skier and explore the deficiencies of character which must destroy him. All these films show TV expanded to fill the needs of cinema rather than any adaptation of the directors to a different medium.

In the same way, Sidney Lumet pursued in his features the approach and style of his Fifties TV drama; *View from the Bridge* (1962, in France) and *Long Day's Journey into Night* (1962), based on Arthur Miller and Eugene O'Neill respectively, use television's intricate camera movements and dramatic lighting. Bogged down by the unfortunate casting of Italian Raf Vallone and newcomer Carol Lawrence, more appropriate in *West Side Story* and other Broadway musicals, the first succeeded only marginally; but good casting for O'Neill's painfully autobiographical play (Katharine Hepburn and Ralph Richardson as drug-addicted mother and haunted father, Jason Robards Jnr. and Dean Stockwell as the sons) and a gloomy style of long unwinding crane shots and shadowy close-ups gave *Long Day's Journey into Night* remarkable force. Few O'Neill adaptations have had such power.

*THE PAWNBROKER: Thelma Oliver*

Curiously uneven, studded with failures like a limp version of Chekhov's *The Sea Gull* (1968), which except for James Mason's Trigorin sank in a wan Edwardian fog, and his disastrous *The Appointment* (1969), Lumet's career swings between insight and affectation. *Fail-Safe* (see Chapter Ten), *The Hill* (1965, in England), a brutal account of a British military prison and the tortures to which tough sergeant Sean Connery is subjected, and *The Pawnbroker* (1965), a commercially and artistically successful drama with Rod Steiger's New York hock-shop owner tortured by memories of the death camps and his failure to save his wife and child, provide a body of serious, if self-consciously "significant" work against which one balances lighter films like *The Group* (1966) and *Bye Bye Braverman* (1968). These latter two, though more superficial, are closer, one senses, to Lumet's true style than the bravura of much-praised sequences like that in *The Pawnbroker* where a Negro prostitute's exposure of her body as a bribe brings flooding back to the man disjointed images of his wife's humiliation in a Nazi officers' brothel. *Bye Bye Braverman*, a fragmentary account of four Jewish friends diverted on their way to the suburban funeral of a fifth, used New York locations and Jewish attitudes in clever contrast, gently parodying Tom Bosley's enthusiastic cineaste who boasts that his John Ford monograph has been reprinted four times, and Joseph Wiseman's stolidly embittered custodian of principles (surely a satire on *The Pawnbroker*'s hero) who refuses to ride in a Volkswagen and paralyses every conversation with reminders of "six million dead." Only George Segal as the vague leading character rises above religion and memory; concerned for life and the future, he makes a touchingly funny address to an enormous cemetery on which they stumble, treating the ranked headstones as an attentive audience. "What can I tell you? Things have changed. Girls are prettier. Boys are uglier — but smarter . . ." Also TV-oriented, *The Group*,

*Sidney Lumet*

from Mary McCarthy's waspish novel of sexual experiment among a group of 1930s Vassar girls, showed Lumet overturning the illusions of stardom to accumulate a cast of eight virtual unknowns, most of whom went on to distinguished careers in the cinema, notably Candice Bergen, Joan Hackett, Elizabeth Hartman, Joanna Pettet and Jessica Walter. Although Sidney Buchman's telescoping of the novel's leisurely development makes the film a mini-Peyton Place in its sexual permutations, Lumet's direction shows both sincerity and restraint. Hand-held shooting by his regular cameraman Boris Kaufman, intricate 360-degree tracks around the girls at a lunch, or through and around the participants in love scenes or domestic arguments, involve one in the action, while a frank stillness for the arrival of Candice Bergen's icy Lesbian or for the agonising "natural" childbirth of Elizabeth Hartman gives even greater emphasis to painful moments. Here, one senses throughout *The Group*, is the essence of TV's potential contribution to the cinema, a style which, when used with the insight of a Lumet or Frankenheimer, can offer new truths about characters who, in the conventional cinema, achieve charisma but not personality.

# 4. Something the Kids Can Whistle

THE CONJUNCTION of music and image, the most powerful in art, was always a high card in the Hollywood pack, and one it used throughout its history with skill. Although most master film composers — Korngold, Steiner, Newman, Victor Young — had died or retired by the Sixties, the "big score" tradition, with dramatic title theme and careful tailoring of music to specific incidents, survived in the work of Miklos Rozsa (*El Cid*, *The Power*) and Alex North (*Cleopatra*, *Spartacus*). But film music in general moved away from this pattern as old composers retired, production shrank and new men the Fifties should have trained failed to appear. As in the case of acting and direction, music departments were forced to look outside the industry, mainly to jazz, where the most inventive new minds in American popular composition had collected. Experience as "session musicians" producing sophisticated arrangements for albums by Frank Sinatra, Tony Bennett and Perry Como gave these men the discipline and consciousness of mood essential to film scoring, and, often after a brief TV apprenticeship, they were quickly hired by Hollywood.

Jazz-oriented scores were not new to American cinema. André Previn had a spell in Hollywood during his rise from jazz pianist to the eminence of orchestral conductor and composer, while the suit of Milton "Shorty" Rogers against Leith Stevens for taking sole music credit on *The Wild One* (1953) whose score Rogers had, as any jazz fan could hear, composed and performed, and the success of Johnny Mandel's music for *I Want to Live* (1958) suggested to the jazz world that a breakthrough was imminent. But although jazz emerged as a dominant influence in Sixties film music, it was jazz softened to the Hollywood image. The symphonic sound of Steiner and Korngold gave way to one more reminiscent of "mood music," a solo instrument weaving simple melodies against a lush background in which jazz sounds were mixed with strings. The style had its best exponents in men like Johnny Mandel, whose theme music for *The Sandpiper*, "The Shadow of Your Smile," combined with sunset helicopter shots of Big Sur cliffs, became one component of a memorable credits sequence, unfortunately betrayed by the flummery that followed.

Total jazz scores were occasionally successful, notably Duke Ellington's for *Anatomy of a Murder*, with the composer in a diffident personal appearance as pianist "Pie Eye" playing four-handed with James Stewart, but a synthesis of jazz and mid-brow classicism usually prevailed. B-movie graduate Henry Mancini, whose jazz themes for the *Peter Gunn* and *Mr. Lucky* TV series enjoyed a period in vogue, subordinated his background to create the unique "Mancini sound," a melody crooned by a small choir over strings of an often cloying sweetness — a style well-suited to the romances of Blake Edwards, with whom he often worked. Title tunes for Edwards's *Breakfast at Tiffany's* ("Moon River"), *The Great Race* ("The Sweetheart Tree"), *Days of Wine and Roses* and Delbert Mann's *Dear Heart*, as well as for Stanley Donen's *Two for the Road*, his best, all met with popular success, but the real Mancini, astringent and dramatic, is more apparent in the jangling electric piano of Howard Hawks's *Hatari!*, the breathy tenor sax and plucked bass of *The Pink Panther* and in the remarkable scene in *A Shot in the Dark* where detective Peter Sellers, investigating murder in a nudist camp, comes upon an entire jazz band, stark naked, pounding out the film's brassy theme.

Among recruits from New York jazz circles, Quincy Jones (*In The Heat of the Night*, *In Cold Blood*), Elia Kazan's *protégé* David Amram (*Splendor in the Grass*, *The Young Savages*, *The Manchurian Candidate*, *The Arrangement*) and Lalo Schifrin (*The Cincinnati Kid*, *Bullitt*) all achieved some eminence, though the success of Jerry Goldsmith and Elmer Bernstein was more remarkable. Bernstein's Fifties scores showed an arresting blend of jazz elements and dissonant strings, particularly in *The Man with the Golden Arm*, and he became increasingly in demand as a composer for action films, his blend of cowboy expansiveness and rattling percussion for *The Magnificent Seven* (reminiscent of the film's Japanese original, *Seven Samurai*) reaching hit-parade popularity. Goldsmith, whose themes for TV's *The Man from U.N.C.L.E.* and *Twilight Zone*, though famous, are inferior to his experimental scores for the horror/suspense programme *Thriller* in which he mixed high-pitched Herrmannesque violins and sudden staccato accents, developed a more personal style than most, well suited to the steely tension of John Frankenheimer, for whom he scored *Seven Days in May* and *Seconds*, two of that director's most cerebral films. But the scores for *A Patch of Blue* (Guy Green, 1965), in which sound clusters evoked the blind girl's only occupation of stringing beads, the blaring horns in *Planet of the Apes* and the dauntingly complex passacaglia created for the air battle sequence of *The Blue Max* (John Guillermin) show a musician of formal skill and authority, with a style to which other composers, including Bernstein in *To Kill a Mockingbird*, paid the compliment of imitation.

While studios were willing to accept background scores of considerable sophistication, their choice of subjects for musicals depended exclusively on budget. Pursuing only that which had a proven commercial pedigree, they discarded original musicals, a staple Hollywood *genre*, for films of Broadway successes. Enormous sums ($5½ million for *My Fair Lady*, $2,100,000 for *Hello Dolly!*) were paid for the film rights to stage hits, an expenditure which, when added to that for costumes, sets and recording, made musicals, always the most costly production in the Hollywood repertoire, more expensive still. As only hard-ticket success could repay such investments, plots were padded and extravagant settings employed to prolong the frailest show. A boom-or-bust mentality prevailed. *My Fair Lady* and *The Sound of Music* revived almost overnight the failing fortunes of Warner Brothers and 20th Century-Fox respectively, but the latter immediately afterwards lost huge amounts with *Star!* and *Doctor Dolittle*. Money fed on money. The $18 million *Doctor Dolittle* needed another $10 million to be promoted and distributed, and the interest on this borrowed $28 million ate up profits as quickly as they accumulated. Only total runaway success could justify the production of a block-buster musical, and after the *Dolittle* failure planned musicals based on "Peter Pan" and the Tom Swift stories were prudently dropped.

Viewed purely as films, a difficult task considering their industrial importance, few of Hollywood's Sixties musicals had great value, artistic honours often going to the least ambitious. Mervyn LeRoy's *Gypsy* (1963) charmingly sugared Gypsy Rose Lee's autobiography, with performances of wit and animation by Natalie Wood as Gypsy, Rosalind Russell as her mother and Karl Malden as an avuncular auxiliary. LeRoy refuses to glamourise his backstage setting or the griminess of Gypsy's rise to become America's top stripper after years as "that three-foot-three bundle of dynamite" in the vaudeville act of Baby June and Company. Few of Jule Styne's numbers are accorded the lavish Hollywood treatment; "You Gotta Have a Gimmick," with seedy strippers in seedier costumes demonstrating their acts, including Mazeppa ("Revolutions in Dance") (Faith Dane) who appears in warrior costume, complete with trumpet, and "Electrifying Electra" (Roxanne Arlen) whose costume lights up at the vital moment, is set in a dressing-room of authentic untidiness, while

*GYPSY: Karl Malden, Natalie Wood, and Rosalind Russell*

"Small World," sung by Russell (dubbed by Lisa Kirk) and Malden in a small-town café, is a quiet and charming romantic interlude perfectly suited to the song. Even Natalie Wood's concluding "Let Me Entertain You" is shot by LeRoy as a theatrical montage showing her graduation from terrified tyro unable to remove any more than her gloves to an experienced professional who sheds only a little more but makes it look like the lot, a scene precisely evocative of burlesque, with hardly a nod at the glamorous conventions of Hollywood.

*Bye Bye Birdie* (1963) and *Viva Las Vegas* (*Love in Las Vegas* in UK) (1964) achieved much with limited resources. The most energetic of Hollywood's musical makers, with the shrill liveliness of *Kiss Me Kate* and *Annie Get Your Gun* to his credit, George Sidney relished these noisy films, with their emphasis on youthful ebullience, and stars (notably his *protégée* Ann-

Margret) whose grasp of acting and pitch was at best problematic. Although Dick Van Dyke as the unsuccessful song-writer and Janet Leigh as his long-suffering *fiancée* stiffen the structure of *Bye Bye Birdie*, well supported by Paul Lynde as a sarcastic father and Maureen Stapleton, horrific in squeaking crêpe-soled shoes, as Van Dyke's clinging mother ("What if he *is* an ingrate, so long as he's happy"), the burden necessarily rests on Ann-Margret as the girl who wins the right to be kissed on national TV by pop star Conrad Birdie, Bobby Rydell as her doubtful boy friend and Jesse Pearson as the randy sub-Presley Birdie — all young players who cave in surprisingly seldom under the weight. Offered as a satire on the generation gap, *Bye Bye Birdie*, except in the acid song "Kids" ("Why can't they be like we were/Perfect in every way?"), seldom lives up to its responsibilities, showing both sides as equally obsessed with sex, the older generation through Janet Leigh's fantasy of multiple seduction in "The Shriners Ballet" and the children in Birdie's arrival to the tune of "One Last Kiss" that reduces the town to frenzy and collapse. An animated 'teenage pin-up, using all the tricks of Jean Harlow without her mocking humour, Ann-Margret brings little to the film, except in a brightly choreographed (Onna White/Tom Panko) "Got a Lotta Living To Do": clad in skin-tight pink pants, leading a wedge of dancers towards the camera in a heavy-eyed evocation of teenage lust, she embodies one vision at least of the emerging generation. *Bye Bye Birdie* contrasts oddly with *Viva Las Vegas*; Ann-Margret again stars, this time as a Las Vegas swimming instructress, in support of Elvis Presley, whose suggestive singing style and wide-spectrum sexual appeal were parodied in the earlier film. Unremarkable in its story of Presley's adventures as a racing driver, culminating in a disastrous race in which crashes outnumber the cars competing, *Viva Las Vegas* gives Sidney the opportunity for some lively numbers: "Come on, Everybody," a song-and-dance for the two stars shot in an empty rehearsal hall, and a fiery version of Ray Charles's "What'd I Say" using the director's cherished image of a circular circus-ring floor pattern with dancers stamping frantically in concentric circles as the Presley style moves into top gear.

As an evocation of modern sexuality, Francis Ford Coppola's *You're a Big Boy Now* (1967) had more validity. Canadian Peter Kastner, excellent in Don Owen's *Nobody Waved Goodbye*, plays confused, frustrated and parent-dominated Bernard Chanticleer, whose move from suburban home to New York apartment brings him into the clutches of off-Broadway actress Barbara Darling (Elizabeth Hartman), with whom he experiences the backlash of her childhood seduction by a fifty-three year old albino hypnotherapist with a wooden leg, of which event a trophy — the leg — hangs over her bed. Musical set-pieces are replaced with a background score by John Sebastian — performed by his group, The Lovin' Spoonful — with which the image is excitingly integrated: Bernard on roller skates coasting around the stacks of the New York Central Library to the film's title tune, and Barbara bursting through the reading room's double doors, camera tracking furiously before her as the frantic "Hey, Beautiful Girl" roars out. Julie Harris as his landlady, Miss Thing, who keeps a pet chicken and is revered by a thuggish cop (Dolph Sweet) who, even when shaving, wears his Police Special, Michael Dunn as Barbara's dwarf biographer and Rip Torn as Bernard's wolfish father, Keeper of Incunabula at the Library, are a supporting cast of eccentric merit while scenes shot in natural light around New York — Bernard, watching a strip-film in a penny arcade machine, gets his tie caught and nearly strangles; he visits a discotheque whose walls writhe in selections from Roger Corman horror movies and Coppola's own *Dementia 13* (1964) (also *The Haunted and the Hunted*), whose production Corman financed — give the film a fine sense of that city's nervous vitality.

Coppola graduated quickly, and by 1968 was directing an adaptation of *Finian's Rainbow*, the Burton Lane/E. Y. Harburg musical about leprechaun Finian McLonergan's search in a mythical American South for his stolen crock of gold. In a style somewhere between Busby Berkeley and Edward Albee, Coppola combines music with satire, taking some accurate shots at racial attitudes: a Negro plant biologist (Al Freeman Jnr.) searching for the secret of the ready-mentholated tobacco plant, slips readily into the role of shuffling old retainer when circumstances demand it, while the film's meagre plot depends on the ability of Fred Astaire's Finian to turn its racialist heavies, Judge Billboard Rawkins and his sons, black. But finally the music proves most impressive, with English *chanteuse* Petula Clark giving an astringent edge to "How Are Things in Glocca Morra?", "Look to the Rainbow" and, most readily remembered, a sexy "Old Devil Moon" sung in wintry moonlight where swooping crane shots convey a tingling erotic fever.

Among Sixties musicals, one missed most the ebullient mid-budget originals which had always been a backbone of the *genre. Singin' in the Rain* and *The Pirate* had few counterparts, and graduates of this lively school were among the recession's saddest casualties. Howard Keel

*MARY POPPINS: Dick Van Dyke, Julie Andrews*

reflectively returned to the stage, and Judy Garland became a ravaged trouper mocking her image with some bitter TV appearances before a premature death in loneliness and despair. The few original musicals of the Sixties were aimed at the teenage and family market, sometimes fatally confusing the two. Among the most successful was Disney's *Mary Poppins* (Robert Stevenson, 1965), from P. L. Travers's popular books for children about an all-powerful nanny and her charges. Julie Andrews in dowdy clothes and magic umbrella was too young for the part, but the film's ingenuity, especially in its combination of live action and animation, smoothed over such errors. Poppins's magic clean-up of the nursery, Dick

49

Van Dyke's rooftop Sweeps Ballet and some energetic dance numbers in the park with cartoon animals are among the most durable scenes of the decade. Also for children, *Doctor Dolittle* (Richard Fleischer, 1968) eschewed animation, often with alarming results; $1 million was spent for animals alone, including a large sum on teaching a chimpanzee to fry bacon and eggs. Rex Harrison, who starred with ill-concealed distaste as Hugh Lofting's super-vet., has since recalled the hygiene problems of working on an over-heated and cramped set with zebras, snakes, sheep and a llama, and the frequent breaks in production needed for cleaning-up and airing (finally a tilting floor and drains were fitted to facilitate these). An ideal choice for the role, Harrison dominates his scenes with aplomb, and the sight of this urbane actor, in top hat and cane, surrounded by a flock of sheep with whom he appears to be carrying on an animated conversation, is one to cherish from an uneven and disastrously uncommercial production.

Despite these few originals, the Broadway adaptation remained the staple Hollywood musical. Shows surviving the transition were rare. *The Unsinkable Molly Brown* (Charles Walters, 1964) made up for indifferent songs and the presence of stolid baritone Harve Presnell with a spirited performance from Debbie Reynolds as a turn-of-the-century rough-diamond hostess who survived, among other disasters, the sinking of the "Titanic." The choreography, of energetic precision, was by TV graduate Peter Gennaro, a lonely example of Hollywood recognising the vitality of pop shows like *Shindig*; unfortunately the romping violence of "Belly up to the Bar, Boys!" was little imitated by a cautious studio establishment. Vincente Minnelli's *The Bells Are Ringing* (1960) belongs more to the Fifties, as does the inimitable Judy Holliday. Shrilling "Sus*answer*phone," crawling around her cluttered apartment/office in an agony of confused languor crooning "I'm in love with a man/Plaza O-double-four-double-three" or prancing through the high-style tableau of "Drop a Name" she contrived both to send up and wring of its melody and wit the Jule Styne/Betty Comden/Adolph Green score. This independent approach to stage musicals succumbed to a fashion merely to copy and expand the original as a means of retaining the Broadway impact. George Cukor's *My Fair Lady* (1964) set the fashion and skilfully exploited the form's limited potential with a flair few later productions were to achieve. Although Audrey Hepburn, Rex Harrison and Stanley Holloway gave a good account of the superb Lerner and Loewe score, much credit for the film's box-office success clearly goes to its designers; production designer Cecil Beaton, and set directors Gene Allen and George James Hopkins. The stately "Ascot Gavotte" with dancers in elaborately recreated Edwardian costumes of black and white pacing in a stylised representation of polite society shows a respect for style audiences instinctively admired.

William Wyler was to have directed a film with Audrey Hepburn as Peter Pan, but this never materialised; the same team was mooted for *The Sound of Music*, with Romy Schneider a possible alternative star, but Julie Andrews, who had missed repeating her role of Eliza Dolittle in *My Fair Lady* after both Cukor and Jack Warner decided a "name" was essential, had her revenge at last in Robert Wise's awesomely profitable 1965 adaptation of Rogers's and Hammerstein's Trapp Family Singers musical, Broadway style finally outweighing Hollywood tradition. Instant and spectacular commercial success — it is now the most profitable film ever made — brought equally immediate critical obloquy, and few writers bothered to find merit in this persuasive and restrained version of a syrupy romance; "We didn't have a tenth the dirndls we could have had," the

*WEST SIDE STORY: George Chakiris*

director said defensively. Exterior handling of the unremarkable songs, and atmospheric use of tunes like "My Favourite Things," sung to calm the children during a thunderstorm, show the imagination of a man whose credentials include some of the cinema's most realistic films, though Wise's skill at combining music with image had been more apparent in *West Side Story* (1961), where his self-effacing direction is an implied tribute to Leonard Bernstein's score and Jerome Robbins's choreography. Planned as a co-direction project with Wise and Robbins, *West Side Story* passed entirely to Wise after the choreographer had shot the film's prologue of dancers leaping and chasing through New York slums, and the songs "America," "Cool" and "I Fell Pretty." Wise claimed Robbins's unfamiliarity with cinema technique led him into excessive cover shooting and an inability to avoid following up any new idea, but since Robbins rehearsed the dancers in all the numbers and left behind two assistants to help Wise, his signature is apparent throughout. Natalie Wood and Richard Beymer lack the impact of their Broadway counterparts, but in ensemble singing and dancing *West Side Story* has few competitors.

Predictably, Wise's most satisfying musical was a financial disaster, hampered by its imagination and good taste. *Star!* (1968) cast Julie Andrews in a romanticised version of Thirties revue star Gertrude Lawrence's life and career. Although Wise captured the ambiance of Broadway and London's West End in which Noël Coward, Alexander Woollcott and Jack Buchanan were magical figures, modern audiences rejected the film completely, ignorant of the names and impatient with the episodic pacing and antique setting accentuated by a pre-credits black-and-white newsreel using the small screen. Even after being extensively cut and retitled *Those Were the Happy Times* (as if to assure audiences that it was gaily nostalgic, a "Thoroughly Modern Gertie"), *Star!* remained an obstinate millstone around 20th Century-Fox's neck. Despite commercial failure, the film is one of Wise's best, featuring elegant versions of Coward's "Half Caste Woman" and "Parisian Pierrot" (early songs which Lawrence, in fact, never sang). Sets and costumes of dusky pink and purple and the use of confined stage settings mock the tasteless circuses of *Hello Dolly!* and *Funny Girl*, though the finale, Kurt Weill's "Poor Jenny" from "Lady in the Dark," contrives to be both lavish and sophisticated. The star's emotional and marital problems are understandably romanticised, but Daniel Massey as a believable Noël Coward hints at her temperament and arrogance. (Coward endorsed the characterisation by his godson Massey, noting only one "grave technical error. He sang better than I did.") *Star!*'s sin was to treat the recent past in the style of its time rather than as a ludicrous anachronism, the fault of George Roy Hill's popular *Thoroughly Modern Millie* (1967), in which Andrews also starred. Wise's London backgrounds are grimly real, a pub's low ceilings, smoke-stained walls and dim mirrors emphasising Gertie's skill as an entertainer when she dominates a noisy crowd by dancing on the bar. Played with a stiffness inconsistent with the original (and marred by ineffective audience "laughs off"), brief extracts from the balcony scene of "Private Lives" and "Has Anybody Seen Our Ship?" from the "Red Peppers" episode of "Tonight at Eight Thirty" still respected Twenties style, baffling modern audiences to whom that decade had come to mean only jazz babies and the Charleston.

Even after studios that had lost on block-buster musicals retired from this risky field, the richer and more obstinate persisted, clinging to the hope that a *genre* that had produced fabulous profits would, by some magical formula nobody understood, eventually do so again. William Wyler's *Funny Girl* (1968) used Barbra Streisand in the role of Fanny Brice she had created, the gaps in Jule Styne's meagre score and Isobel Lennart's equally threadbare book being filled with additional romantic detail, necessarily compromised by the necessity to sweeten Miss Brice's involvement with gambler Nicky Arnstein and his conviction for fraud. Despite this plastic surgery, *Funny Girl* depends on a chorus-girl-to-star plot outdated even by the time of *Forty-Second Street*, one into which Wyler, stars Streisand and Omar Sharif, and dance director Herbert Ross cannot breathe life. Only the end of the "Don't Rain on My Parade" number, shot from a helicopter as Fanny stands on the bow of a tug pursuing Nicky's liner out of New York harbour, recalls Wyler's proven skill as a screen romantic. Barbra Streisand also starred in *Hello Dolly!* (Gene Kelly, 1970), an adaptation of Thornton Wilder's *The Matchmaker*, already filmed — without music — in 1958, but again a thin score (Jerry Herman) forced the director to emphasise a framing story to which producer/scenarist Ernest Lehman added much additional material. Fortunately, the plot of Nineties New York widow Dolly Levi whose matchmaking activities are directed mainly towards catching for herself the rich misogynistic Horace Vandergelder, is strong enough to bear the weight under which *Funny Girl* sagged. Walter Matthau perfectly characterises the canny, expostulating merchant, eclipsing even Paul Ford's playing in the earlier version with a range of splutters, mutters and double takes awesome in its variety. Unfortunately the need to expand the simplest situation leads to "Before the Parade Passes By" being embedded in an horrifically vulgar patriotic parade against a convincingly recreated (at a cost for one set of $1.6 million) Nineties New York, and "Hello Dolly" being given an interminable treatment in the Harmonia Gardens restaurant, Streisand flanked by acrobatic waiters and Louis Armstrong dragooned into singing his hit version of the title song. On the other hand, "Put On Your Sunday Clothes," with Michael Kidd's dancers prancing in the sunlight around an excursion train recalls the energy Kelly as a dancer brought to his classic musicals of the Fifties.

An agreeable exception to the vulgarity of Broadway show films, *Sweet Charity* (1969) boasted a script by the skilled Peter Stone from Fellini's *La Notte di Cabiria*, and Shirley MacLaine brings humour and feeling to Giulietta Masina's original role of the lonely prostitute whose hope for a better life survives squalour, deprivation and unrequited love. Cy Coleman and Dorothy Fields provide a routine score, enlivened mainly by the direction of Bob Fosse, agile second-lead dancer of Fifties film musicals and since then a talented Broadway choreographer/director. His imagination adds sparkle to the dullest numbers, and genuine depth to set-pieces like "Hey, Big Spender," with dance hall girls draped over a rail, languidly encouraging the attention of patrons in a scene that has a stinging sense of the bought and their contempt for the buyer. "There's Gotta Be Something Better Than This," musically similar to *West Side Story*'s "America" even to the rooftop setting, gets an even more frenzied treatment than Robbins provided, and "Rich Man's Frug," a clever parody of pop dancing in high-life clubs with expressionless socialites jerking and gliding through starkly modernistic sets, is genuinely original in conception. Reviving a practice common in the Fifties, the studio offered exhibitors a choice of endings, one where Charity, abandoned by her lover, wanders off with some flowers hippies have offered to her as a symbol of continuing hope, and a second in which he returns for a last-minute reunion. Neither, regretfully, made *Sweet Charity* show any profit.

Satirist Mel Brooks said the last word on musicals in his *The Producers* (1968), which he also produced and wrote. Sinking a knife lovingly into the boom-or-bust philosophy of musical production, he deflated at the same time the form's rejection of talent in favour of gimmickry. Accountant Gene Wilder discovers that his boss, Broadway producer Zero Mostel, has been swindling his aged lady backers, accepting investments for shows that are never produced. The plot uncovered, they amalgamate to present the

*"Hey, Big Spender" from SWEET CHARITY*

most disastrously unsuccessful show they can devise, a musical biography of Hitler, hoping that in the resulting ruin the backers will not realise that 2,500% of the show has been sold. Unfortunately, it succeeds, and both partners end up in jail. With this frail plot, already the basis of at least one film (*Curtain Call*, Frank Woodruff, 1940) Brooks demolishes the musical's pretensions and idiocies: the camp director mincing in drag to the astonishment of his employers, the parade of hopeful Hitlers blandly turning up for auditions in toothbrush moustaches, and Dick Shawn as an unlikely lead stopping the audition (and the film) with a tormented pop protest about what a cop did to the flower he offered him in the street. At the finale, as the title tune of "Springtime for Hitler" unrolls with Busby Berkeley patterns of dancers in the form of a swastika, a parade of goose-stepping chorus girls and models clad in pretzels and beer steins, the full ludicrousness of the inflated Sixties musical becomes all too clear, a form on which Hollywood's reliance proved the worst error of a disastrous period.

# 5. After Alfred

NAMES TO conjure with occur seldom in the cinema, and Hollywood had cause to regret that Alfred Hitchcock, its most potent innovator but plagued by short-sighted studios and lazy audiences, devoted himself in the Sixties to personal statement. Films were needed to rival his slick thrillers of the Fifties — *Vertigo, Rear Window, North by Northwest* — and Hollywood duly developed a new school of adventure films to order. Ian Fleming's suave spy romances engendered both the idea, of action fantasies well salted with violence and sex, and their central character, the handsome, amoral and coldly efficient "agent." While it was a cause for regret around the studios that British-based producers Harry Saltzman and Albert "Cubby" Broccoli had bought up almost all Fleming's original novels before anybody else saw their film potential, they responded to money-makers like *Doctor No* (1962), *From Russia with Love* (1964), *Thunderball* (1966, all by Terence Young) and Guy Hamilton's witty, crackling *Goldfinger* (1964), best of the bunch, with films on sub-Fleming characters like Donald Hamilton's Matt Helm, the men from U.N.C.L.E (Robert Vaughn and David McCallum recreating their TV roles), and the Flint films in which James Coburn, most menacing of Fifties heavies, was elevated to star status. The resulting snob thrillers offered audiences the action, sex and high fashion they had found in the musical before it adopted Broadway modes, and the Western before it got a conscience.

Among those who shrewdly pounced on Hitchcock's leftovers, Stanley Donen's *Charade* (1964) set a durable fashion in chic thrillers (and one-word titles); *Mirage, Masquerade* (Basil Dearden, 1966, in UK), *Arabesque, Kaleidoscope, Caprice* and *Blindfold* followed. Many shared the theme of Ernest Lehman's *North by Northwest* script, in which a rich, glamorous professional man — psychiatrist, academic, tycoon — is lured from his comfortable life, often by a woman, and finds himself a pawn in some elaborate plot. The villain is usually cultured and foreign, the setting for these adventures a European country and the conclusion, after a bizarre chase, bloody. Peter Stone's *Charade* script played all the Hitchcockian possibilities from the early scene of socialite Audrey Hepburn sunning herself at an alpine resort, a gun emerging in a gloved hand and filling her ear with water from a child's water-pistol. Subsequently she finds her Paris flat stripped of its furniture, her husband, after his sudden death while fleeing

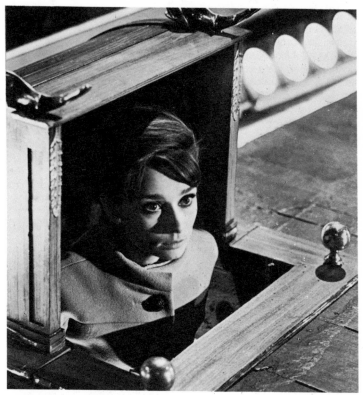

*CHARADE: Audrey Hepburn*

the country, is revealed as an international criminal, and a grim group of Americans involve her in their search for a fortune in gold they and her husband stole during the war. Calmly romancing the widow and representing himself variously as thief, vengeful relative, FBI agent and tax investigator, Cary Grant manages well in a role essentially the reverse of that in *North by Northwest*, where *he* was the innocent in love with somebody about whose motives and honesty he was continually in doubt. Except for an idyll on the Seine in a glass-roofed floating restaurant, Donen wisely avoids plush salons and tourist spots, setting the action in a convincingly ramshackle Latin Quarter hotel and the untidy clutter of the Tuileries. Hitchcock's black humour is evident in the villains' characterisation: George Kennedy is a hook-handed sadist, and James Coburn the folksily sinister Tex Penthollow, who jabs a corpse's hand with a pin to make sure that it is dead and terrorises Hepburn in a phone box by dropping lighted matches into her lap (a role which was to be a signpost to Coburn's later eminence in a series of roles culminating in Flicker's picaresque *The President's Analyst*).

*Arabesque* (1966), for which Donen repeated the exercise in London, set philologist Gregory Peck against Alan Badel's Levantine villain with Sophia Loren as the prize. More free-wheeling and violent than *Charade*, it capitalised on Loren's opulent beauty, having her and Peck share

*MIRAGE: Gregory Peck, Diane Baker*

58

a shower in order to carry on a private conversation, and giving the star some extreme Dior fashions, all navel-deep necklines and pink vinyl. Shrewdly, Donen emphasises the plot's Middle-Eastern ruthlessness by frequent references to wild animals and birds of prey; after an atmospheric chase through London Zoo at night, animals shrieking and roaring at the torches, the climax occurs in the Aquarium, where light shimmers on the walls, two men wrestle above a tank of sharks and the room is flooded with water and wriggling fish as bullets shatter the glass. Badel's villain is wickedly acid. Peck, about to feed his pet hawk a date, is warned against it: "Flesh, Mr. Pollock. He only eats flesh." "Really? I thought he looked a little hungry just then." "It must have been your fingers," Badel suggests.

Peck again starred in *Mirage* (1965), directed by Edward Dmytryk with another Peter Stone script. An exercise in the ambiguities of memory and one whose harsh black and white style recalls Dmytryk's Forties success as director of *Farewell My Lovely*, it involves chemist Peck in a killing he cannot remember. Ingeniously elaborate in its use of city landscape, *Mirage* has a Chinese Puzzle fascination for devotees, though many audiences on its first release found themselves left behind in the shifting levels of reality. A good deal more direct, Philip Dunne's *Blindfold* (1966), which the veteran scenarist also wrote, with W. H. Menger, cast Rock Hudson as a New York psychoanalyst and Claudia Cardinale as the sister of a scientist kidnapped by enemy agents. Whisked to a hideout to treat the man for mental disturbance, Hudson later guides the FBI there by piecing together aural clues picked up during the trip. If one accepts Hudson as an analyst, no lesser suspension of disbelief can be strained at, and on this basis *Blindfold* is an agreeable entertainment. Two years later, the same stars came together in Italy for *Ruba al Prossimo Tuo* (*A Fine Pair* elsewhere), in which Hudson is a New York cop helping jewel thief Cardinale to break into a villa and return the loot she took; the gimmick of heating the house to an almost fatal temperature to immobilise its burglar alarms gives a unique erotic interest to the sequence, director Francesco Maselli using the perspiration-bathed break-in to inject a sexual interest at which *Blindfold* merely hinted.

Among the Sixties' most successful films, Blake Edwards's *The Pink Panther* and *A Shot in the Dark* (both 1964) were comedy-thrillers with the accent on humour, chic settings and elegant foreign female stars (Cardinale for *The Pink Panther*, Elke Sommer for *A Shot in the Dark*, where she replaced Loren as Edwards had replaced Anatole Litvak) combined with

*THE GREAT RACE: Natalie Wood*

the Keatonesque comedy of inanimate objects in which Edwards has few masters. As in *The Great Race* (1965), Edwards's Nineties romp about a long-distance car race, sight gags bear the entire weight of both films. *A Shot in the Dark* opens with an elaborate sequence seen through the windows of a French chateau, with elegant figures in silk dressing gowns slipping from room to room, the whole culminating in a murder. Peter Sellers's Inspector Clouseau bumbles through both in traditional private-eye gear, falling into ponds, setting himself alight, and ripping the baize of billiard tables with a furious incompetence into which all are drawn. In *The Pink Panther*, Robert Wagner, neophyte nephew of David Niven's cultivated jewel thief, finds himself trapped in Clouseau's apartment with the inspector's wife (Capucine), where he becomes submerged in the bath or spreadeagled on the pivoting door of the linen cupboard (which flips him into sight and out again before he is noticed — a Keaton gag cribbed from *Sherlock Jr.*). Herbert Lom's twitchy police commissioner in *A Shot in the Dark*, spooked by Clouseau, slices off the end of his finger in a guillotine-shaped cigar-cutter and, nervously folding his arms, stabs himself with a letter-opener. At Clouseau's instigation, the world of inanimate objects seems to have turned on man. Even though Edwards respects the form of the Hitchcock thriller, in *The Pink Panther* double-dealing and disguises take over at last, carloads of thieves, police and hangers-on, most of them in fancy dress, meeting in a multiple collision at the centre of a tiny village, witnessed only by a curious peasant who, after many vain attempts to cross the road, resignedly brings out his chair to watch the fun in comfort. Edwards's careful skill has led from a logical premise to heights of absurdity; few directors could have made convincing the scene in *The Pink Panther* where a thief dressed in a full-length gorilla suit opens a wall safe, looks through and sees, opening the safe's other door, another thief in a full-length gorilla suit.

*The Party* (1968), though not a thriller, relies like *The Pink Panther*, on sight-gags and minimal dialogue. Sellers is an inept Indian actor invited by accident to a Hollywood party, which he reduces to total confusion by his fumbling. Again, matter goes wild. Sellers loses his shoe crossing the ornamental pool, sees it caught on a tray of canapes and travel around the room unnoticed by chatting guests until the maid diffidently offers it to him once more. Wandering through the house, he opens one closet to find it stuffed with musicians and marijuana smoke; "Cloza door, man," somebody growls. Behind another door he discovers the butler, clad only in red briefs, practicing muscle-man poses before the mirror. Edwards, then busy getting together *Darling Lili* (1970), his unsuccessful First World War spy romance with a miscast Julie Andrews (by then Mrs. Edwards), gave little attention to *The Party*, but its comedy is fresh and inventive. Another of his Sixties films, now almost forgotten, *Gunn* (1967) adapted the *Peter Gunn* TV series he had produced, and sometimes directed, years earlier. Wooden-faced Craig Stevens plays the role he created in a plot parodying the private-eye *genre*; an obligatory stunning by the villain is administered with a squash ball, the background is high-camp San Francisco society, the *dénouement* set amid shattering mirrors in a plush apartment with the killer revealed as a drag queen. Edwards again uses our consciousness of the thriller mythology. Just as Clouseau calls for his "official detective inspector's macintosh," so Gunn in approved private-eye style quips with police chief Edward Asner (one misses the TV series' Herschel Bernardi), and later a

*GUNN: Blake Edwards*

cop says wearily to another, "Watch him, he's been doing these routines with Peter Gunn downtown."

Like Edwards an instinctive Hollywood stylist, Norman Jewison used wide-screen and Technicolor's cloying pastels with a flair older directors could never achieve. *The Thomas Crown Affair* (1968), which might have been retitled "Playboy Robs a Bank," was the lushest of high-crime thrillers, Steve McQueen, in his nervous athleticism the most powerful of Sixties stars, meeting Faye Dunaway, Penn's popular Bonnie Parker, in a confrontation between financier bandit and career tax investigator as potent in its evocation of new myths as *Bonnie and Clyde* had been. The precision of Jewison's commercial judgement disarms criticism. Whether moping in his yellow sailplane to Michel Legrand's Oscar-winning "The Windmills of Your Mind" or succumbing to Dunaway in a suggestive chess game, all lips, fingers and phallic bishops, McQueen characterises a modern variation on the unhappy aristocrat, and Dunaway an equally traditional clever commoner who almost wins her prince at the end. The superficialities both of theme and style, summed up in trendy split-screen sequences, betray a film which Irving Thalberg would not have been ashamed to produce.

Jack Smight's *Kaleidoscope* (1966), recently re-released as *The Bank Breaker*, is more imaginative than Jewison's film, and also exploits a more provocative sexual object in the tempting Susannah York, pursued across Europe in the course of his professional gambling activities by a casual Warren Beatty, who has the card-sharping brainwave of breaking into the printers' factory and marking the plates themselves. Smight's approach is characteristically flip. Beatty, after a cat-burglar entry into the factory, works with a transistor radio blaring pop into his ear, and police inspector Clive Revill spends his days playing with toy engines in his office or cheating his camp helper Murray Melvin at cards, using an enormous glass to read Beatty's marks. Lurid colour effects, in line with the title, give the film a feel of fantasy, complemented by Eric Porter's narcissistic gambler villain and the moated grange in which an obligatory final chase is set. Also shot in Europe, Ernest Lehman's Hitchcockian script for *The Prize* (Mark Robson, 1963) makes pleasant use of Stockholm locations in a comedy/ drama version of Irving Wallace's portmanteau novel about high-jinks in the selection of Nobel Prize winners. As hard-bitten American novelist and his Swedish translator, Paul Newman and Elke Sommer rightly play their roles with tongue in cheek, and one cherishes the scene of their sudden arrival at a nudist's convention, with a hall of naked listeners turning curiously as they burst in. (Another unexpected appearance was that of Sacha Pitoëff as a killer, recently on screens elsewhere as "M" in *L'Année Dernière à Marienbad*.)

Spy comedy-dramas were, like *The Prize*, as good as their stars. Playing Matt Helm, Dean Martin shambled through four films (*The Silencers*, Phil Karlson, 1966; *Murderer's Row* (1966) and *The Ambushers* (1967) both by Henry Levin; and *The Wrecking Crew* (Phil Karlson, 1969), refreshed in each by a *corps* of nubile and sexually insatiable beauties in Ziegfeld costumes (including a secretary — Beverley Adams — named "Lovey Kravezit") and menaced by grotesque villains, the best of them an obese Chinese spy in *The Silencers* played by the Sixties' Laird Cregar, Victor Buono. (In general, Karlson's versions showed more wit and flair than those by Levin.)

Sharing the Matt Helm films' confusion between comedy and parody, Frank Tashlin's *Caprice* (1967) took the Ross Hunter pattern of Doris Day's assertive career girl and a competitive romance, in this case with a

*THE SILENCERS: Dean Martin, and Stella Stevens*

ludicrously youthful Richard Harris, for a thriller comedy on industrial espionage in the cosmetics trade. Occasional Tashlinesque touches were swamped in the high-life background of Californian bungalows and European ski resorts, while his skill with action likewise succumbed to a routine script, its flatness summed up in Day's reaction to the news that she must extract the secret of a new preparation from a rival group. "In that case," she says with gritted teeth, "I'll be the spy who came in from the cold cream." Funnier, and a genuine satire on the spy *genre* which the Helm films and *Caprice* merely attacked with bladders, *Who Was That Lady?* (George Sidney, 1960) benefited from a sharp script by Norman Krasna. Caught kissing another girl by wife Janet Leigh, fast-talker Tony Curtis and friend Dean Martin invent the tale that they are part-time FBI agents investigating a big case, of which seducing the girl was a part. Although Leigh is fooled, especially after Curtis has a "secret identification" tattooed on his foot (silent comedian Snub Pollard has a clever bit part as the tattooist), the plan backfires when real spies overhear the plotters. At the climax, Curtis and Martin, doped by the enemy and locked in the basement of a big hotel, assume they are on a Russian submarine, open valves to let in the ocean (merely draining the hotel's water supply into the cellar) and are linked, arms around one another, singing "God Bless America" with water rising around their knees, as firemen burst in. Acidly satirical, as one expects from Krasna, and with a testy performance from the skilful James Whitmore as a (genuine) government agent, *Who Was That Lady?* pre-led its field.

As Lee Marvin dominated the annihilating melodrama, reverse of these superficial comedy adventures, James Coburn personified a key figure of spy dramas, the intellectual killer and philosopher assassin who answers the questions Marvin can barely formulate. As early as 1960, in *The Magnificent Seven*, Coburn impressed as a tensely efficient knife-man and gunslinger, using his skill sparingly but with deadly effect. As a long pistol shot brings down a fleeing rider, his young colleague praises his aim. "That was the best shot I ever saw!" Coburn sheathes his gun, disgusted. "It was the *worst* shot. I aimed for the horse." After supporting success in this film, *Charade* and others, Coburn starred in *Our Man Flint* (Daniel Mann, 1966) and *In Like Flint* (Gordon Douglas, 1967), parodies of the agent film with Coburn as an operative of z.o.w.i.e (Zonal Organisation World Intelligence Espionage) accompanied by a Helm-like portable harem. *Our Man Flint* faced him with a secret society whose watch-dog was a bald eagle trained only to attack Americans, but though the pattern of guns, girls and gadgetry was stock, Coburn's characterisation was not. When he displays a cigarette lighter and says "It has fifty-eight different functions. Fifty-nine if you want to light a cigarette" our knowledge that such an implement could never exist does not neutralise our belief in Flint's ability to find death-dealing properties in any object, the professional relish of the phrasing suggesting a personality only danger can trigger. Occasionally, action speaks louder than logic. Walking along an office corridor, Flint suddenly demolishes two apparently innocent guards with a fury of karate chops. "They were wearing the ribbon of the Battle of Midway," he explains to an astonished superior. "But . . . there *is* no ribbon of the Battle of Midway." "Precisely," Flint replies. Coburn's personality was exploited cleverly by writer S. Lee Pogostin (*Synanon*, *Pressure Point*), in whose first film as a director, *Hard Contract* (1969), he starred as a professional assassin hired to kill three men hiding in Spain, a search in which the killer shows himself to be as much moralist as murderer, a man whose conversations and relation-

ships during the hunt become complex commentaries on the contemporary obsession with violence. Pogostin's static camera and eccentric direction irked critics who find the thriller form incompatible with serious discussion, but a balanced estimate places *Hard Contract* with Gordon Wiles's forgotten classic *The Gangster*, sharing not only a directorial obsession with Goya, his morbid delight in violent death and relish for the torero/murderer who kills without pity, but the same ambiguous sexual morality that leads Wiles's gangster to sacrifice himself for the love of a vapid beauty and Pogostin's Cunningham to use prostitutes, in whose businesslike rejection of emotion he finds security. In *Duffy* (Robert Parrish, 1968), shot with an English cast and crew in North Africa, and reflecting Morocco's languid atmosphere, Coburn plays a phlegmatic ex-criminal drop-out caught up in the plot of three trendy London *flâneurs*, including James Fox and a delectable Susannah York, to rob the former's father (James Mason) of a Mediterranean bullion shipment. Coburn's Duffy, one of the Sixties archetypal personae, expresses through the appurtenances of his life, mainly a Tangier home cluttered with his own collages and junk sculpture, a total immersion in self, the central calm of a storm, just as his first appearance, tramping over a desert dune into the luxury of an ocean-side club crowded with the brown and indolent rich as Lou Rawls's "I'm Satisfied" bawls on the sound track, shows his superiority, both as thief and human being, to the amateurs in whose plot he becomes involved.

Calm also marks his appearance in *The President's Analyst* (1967) as New York psychoanalyst Sidney Schaefer, dispensing high-priced advice and meditatively banging a gong between appointments. His cool is unruffled even by the announcement of his patient Don Masters (Godfrey Cambridge) that he has just killed an Albanian in the garment district (the film's opening scene, Cambridge in fright wig and "Dizzy Gillespie for President" sweat-shirt stabbing the man, dumping his corpse on a passing trolley of dresses to be whisked away). Asked "Should I feel guilty?", Schaefer says pontifically "No. Killing is an excellent way of dealing with a hostility problem." Cambridge then explains he is an agent of the government and that Schaefer has been chosen to become analyst to the President of the USA. Dazzled, he is whisked, with his girlfriend, to Washington and installed in an apartment on constant call to the White House. When

*DUFFY: James Coburn*

reason begins to sag under the pressure and his girl starts taping his nightly mutterings, Schaefer drops out and hides with a group of hippies, pursued by countless foreign governments as well as America's own Federal Bureau of Regulation whose five-foot high operatives parody the FBI's Hoover-sized spies. Eluding them all, Schaefer encounters the final enemy, the Telephone Company, now controlled by robots who, incensed at the constant complaints about the service, propose to take over the world.

Theodore J. Flicker, leader of Chicago's "Second City" satire troupe and owner of the Premise Club in New York (his first film, *The Trouble-maker*, 1964, is grotesquely funny about the problems of opening a night club in New York), gives *The President's Analyst* a satiric edge. Schaefer, the calm professional, feels logic crumbling as he faces the idiocy of government and the cold war, finding peace only among the hippies. As he makes love to his new girl in a wheat field, and a balloon carries off her discarded dress in a tiny symbol of the ease of peaceful existence, rival spies exterminate each other among the grain, leaving the lovers undisturbed.

*THE PRESIDENT'S ANALYST: James Coburn, Will Geer*

The Quantrills, "a typical American couple," parody middle-class obsessions with status and violence. Attacked in the street, the husband (William Daniels) whips out a pistol to kill his man with professional expertise while his karate-chopping wife demolishes the other. They profess "liberal" politics, "but nothing on the left wing, mind you. The Bullocks — real fascists — ought to be gassed." As American and Russian spies respectively, Negro Godfrey Cambridge and Severn Darden (the latter Flicker's associate in the "Second City" team), give a tight ensemble performance, friendly rivals united in wise-cracking contempt for the game, placing bets on who will be killed first. Cambridge, one of the Sixties' great comic discoveries, has some of the film's best scenes, including his first interview with Schaefer, in which he recalls his school days and the chorus of "Run, run, here comes the nigger" which his friends and eventually he himself took up, a classic encapsulation of the Negro's dilemma in American society. But finally Coburn, as the unflappable technician woken to the emptiness of his expertise by an insane world, dominates the film. At his best, Coburn re-works the figure Gary Cooper characterised in American cinema, the man of honour and private worth, but in his case political conservatism gives way to a modern impatience with dogma, and Cooper's frontier ruthlessness to a thoughtful acceptance and understanding of the politics of violence.

# 6. Cream and Bastards

WHILE THE major studios created sugar-coated confections with thriller fillings, enlivened by the occasional hard centre of a *Duffy* or *Mirage*, more thoughtful (and poorer) companies were exploring other answers to the growing taste for sex, violence and excitement. In the general trend to inflate forms and talents already in existence, producers hit on the private-eye thriller as a profitable subject for exploitation. Such films took on unaccustomed status and scope, and series TV was looted of its best talents — Jack Smight, Buzz Kulik, Stuart Rosenberg — to provide New York atmosphere for some naturalistic detective stories. The new form's preoccupations were summed up in Jack Smight's *Harper* (1966) (*The Moving Target* in UK), where Paul Newman enunciated the morality of the modern private eye. "The bottom's full of nice people;" he remarks, "only cream and bastards rise" — the suggestion that the two categories are synonymous echoing the Sixties willingness, confirmed by the decay of society, to believe that might was right. Declining to explore the consequences of this formulation, Hollywood traded on it with violent and garish thrillers in which only allegiances based on power had any real meaning.

Neither the style nor its ethics were new, both being implicit in Raymond Chandler's novels, if not in the films made from them in the Forties, but Smight's version of Ross Macdonald Chandler's shows the new emphasis on the private eye's charismatic character, and consequent suppression of the social criticism for which many of the books were vehicles. The California of Philip Marlowe is half an illusion, its people "characters," the background against which they move porous, devoid of detail that might lure the reader from significant confrontations. (In this area at least, Paul Bogart's 1969 adaptation of "The Little Sister," *Marlowe*, with a plump and unlikely James Garner in the title role, is accurate. The backgrounds are as empty and insignificant as Stirling Silliphant's uncharacteristically vapid script, but the emptiness is that of pulp fiction, not Chandler's sparse economy). Newman's slouching insolence fits Smight's conception of the Sixties private eye, and the religious cults, high life and seduction against which Harper searches for the kidnapped husband of mantis-like socialite Lauren Bacall ingeniously reflects its time. A fluid style, including some vertiginous helicopter shots, blended with Harper's functional wisecracking, the whole coloured with a personal loneliness and despair, stirs the mire at the bottom of modern society, with Harper the relentless explorer using every trick he knows to discover the truth. One easily believes that the Harper who squeezes information from Shelley Winters's maudlin drunk ("Are you a nice man?" she quavers. "Ma'am, ah don' know if ahm a nice man, but big dawgs lick mah hand") is the same man who visits his estranged wife (Janet Leigh) to beg for the comfort his life now lacks, since central to his philosophy is a need to prove himself as the Chandleresque "man who is not himself mean." His role demonstrates Chandler's famous delineation in "The Simple Art of Murder" of the archetypal urban wolf. Harper would, we sense, "make love to a countess," or at least to Lauren Bacall, and does in fact refuse to oblige virgin Miranda (Pamela Tiffin), despite her provocation, and a gesture, shrewdly chosen by Smight, of drawing a cushion under her hips while encouraging Harper's attention from her father's aphrodisiacally designed circular bed.

Smight, whose background includes episodes of *East Side West Side*, the TV series on a social worker (George C. Scott) in New York's sleazier sections, instinctively understands relationships among a city's cynics. Harper's friendship with attorney Albert Graves (Arthur Hill) is playfully competitive, emphasised when Graves, who loves Miranda, is brushed off in favour of Harper. As the doleful attorney, who has recommended to his friend the value of isometric exercises, watches the couple leave, Harper turns with a grin and makes one of the arm exercises described, a gesture that not only jokes "More exercise" but signals a friendly "I won this time. Your turn next." And at the conclusion, when Graves is revealed as the unwilling perpetrator of the crime Harper has been investigating, the moral conflict does not rack him with doubt but merely interrupts the game. Leaving Graves's car to report it, Harper intentionally exposes his back to a shot, but his friend refuses to fire. Throwing up his hands with an exasperated cry, Harper half spins around and Smight freezes on the gesture, leaving us with the detective's conflicting loyalties and his annoyance that Graves retains too much human feeling to end the game under the new rules.

Smight's other films exhibit the same refusal to rely on conventional characterisation. In *The Third Day* (1965), George Peppard's amnesiac factory-manager is helped back to memory and control of the firm by his estranged wife (Elizabeth Ashley) whose confidence he gains simply by taking her to bed — *in amore veritas*. With a rural high-life setting which conveys, except in an eccentrically original party held in a riding school amid pacing horses, a glossily unreal air, the film's interest is largely in its relationships. Cop Robert Webber hounds Peppard because they were schoolboy rivals, and Roddy McDowall's boardroom opposition is more psychopathic than commercial. *No Way to Treat a Lady* (1968), a *tour de force* for Rod Steiger as a chameleon mass-murderer of women, with personae ranging from hearty Irish priest to camp wig salesman (the latter allowing him the famous retort to the charge that he is a homosexual, "That doesn't mean to say you aren't a nice person"), implies a curious obsession with the case on the part of investigator George Segal, and delineates his odd romance with witness Lee Remick, whose cynical account of her previous love life during a ferry ride on New York harbour encapsulates the film's city cynicism. Although neither were thrillers, *The Secret War of Harry Frigg* (1968) (simply *Frigg* in some places) and *The Illustrated Man* (see Chapter Ten) also discard the obvious. In the first, Paul Newman, archetypal finagling GI, is smuggled into an Italian castle where five Allied generals, content to sit out the war in Nazi-provided luxury, must be encouraged to face their responsibilities, an echo of the theme, common to many Sixties action films, that traditions must give way to force and expediency.

Such films, glamorising the urban wolf, replaced the realistic, black-and-white location crime films common in the Fifties, but the school persisted. *Seven Thieves* (1960) allowed Henry Hathaway to ring some changes on the "big caper" theme with a cantankerously professional Edward G. Robinson leading an audacious casino raid, and in *The List of Adrian Messenger* (1963) John Huston offered an anachronistic but entertaining "gentleman detective" story, George C. Scott hamming cheerfully as the bowler-hatted ex-spymaster investigating a murder plot that threatens to expunge a line of horsey Irish peers. Reflecting Huston's devotion to Ireland, where for most of the Sixties he owned a castle, the film relies for novelty on the gimmick of stars like Robert Mitchum, Frank Sinatra and Burt Lancaster playing bit parts in heavy disguise, then Revealing All at the conclusion, though it was whispered that only Mitchum actually appeared in the routine action attributed to him, a suggestion borne out by the fact that he of all the stars is the only one recognisable.

Not only the crime film but the criminal biography faded. *Murder Inc.* (Stuart Rosenberg and Burt Balaban, 1960) described the Forties investigation by Thomas Dewey and his deputy Burton Turkus into New York

*THE LIST OF ADRIAN MESSENGER: George C. Scott, Dana Wynter*

racketeering that uncovered the murder ring of the title. Their film has the authentic feel of big-time crime, with Peter Falk memorable as the arrogant, almost playful informer Abe Reles, and a plot journalistically faithful to the events it depicts, though less powerful than Raoul Walsh's *The Enforcer* (1951) which dealt with the same incident. In Budd Boetticher's *The Rise and Fall of Legs Diamond* (1960) Ray Danton as the quick and quirky Thirties gangster captures Diamond's insane confidence and Gatsbyesque cool. Classic crime had its shrewdest modern chronicler in Roger Corman, whose *The St. Valentine's Day Massacre* (1967) and *Bloody Mama* (1969), avoiding the documentary accuracy of *Murder Inc.*, offered new and unique interpretations of banditry and the underworld. Jason Robards's Capone is a Machiavellian politician who enjoys and respects power, and the massacre a manoeuvre handled with the calm objectivity of a company takeover. Shelley Winters as Ma Barker in *Bloody Mama* leads a criminal career that, though having little in common with the Barker gang's real

73

*BLOODY MAMA: Don Stroud, Diane Varsi*

exploits, allows Corman and scenarist Robert Thom to explore the sexuality latent in any family relationship; tongue in cheek, the film is dedicated "To The Mothers of America." Corman sets the Barkers' murder, rape, kidnapping and incest against scenes of rural beauty, implying that the potential for acts of inhumanity exists in the quietest social institution, a point underlined by the picnic crowds that gather to watch the final gun battle, but more subtly when Diane Varsi, naked after rising from the bed of Herman (Don Stroud), mocks Lloyd (Robert de Niro) who has spied on them, inviting him to "have a bite of my pie crust. It'd melt in your mouth." One wonders what "Good Housekeeping" would think.

But even Corman's films relate to the Fifties. *The Killers* (Don Siegel, 1964, officially *Ernest Hemingway's The Killers* to avoid confusion with Robert Siodmak's 1946 production) marked the end of the crime documentary, to be superseded by highly coloured fantasies of power. Siegel and actor Lee Marvin crystallised the Sixties gangster movie — flip, artificial, hinged on a poetic use of violence. The most thoughtful of crime film-makers, Siegel, like Smight, declines to accept morality at the current valuation, preferring to show that, like personal relationships, the only durable rules are those agreed among equals. To him, corruption and sudden death are so common and essential to modern life that they cannot be wrong. A morality of force alone prevails. If, Siegel argues, "Do unto others before they do it to you" has become the new golden rule, even this can have its morality if men are prepared to respect the philosophy it implies. Asked to make a TV film from Hemingway's story, screenwriter Gene Coon, like Siodmak, took only the idea of a victim who chooses not to run but passively awaits his murder. Killers Lee Marvin and Clu Gulager, relaxed professionals who enjoy their work, are intrigued by the unwillingness of John Cassavetes to run from them, Marvin exploring this unseemly variation in the logic of existence until he discovers at its source the joker of sex, a random element he understands and is contemptuous of. Shot and

*Richard Widmark and Michael Dunn (left): MADIGAN*

*Don Siegel (standing) directs Susan Clark (right) in COOGAN'S BLUFF*

dying, he raises his gun towards Angie Dickinson, the key to the mystery, and, as she attempts to exercise her attraction over him as she had over others, wearily shakes his head. "Lady," he says, "I haven't got the time," shoots her and dies. When this unique parable, with its casual murderers in conservative suits and dark glasses, its flippant view of violent death and nihilistic new philosophy horrified its sponsors, Siegel, who also produced the film, obtained a successful cinema release. His career, then flagging, had a strong boost, and Lee Marvin emerged as the Sixties' first heavy star.

After *The Killers*, Siegel's position was assured as the most important of thriller directors. With *Madigan* (1968), to whose script blacklisted writer Abraham Polonsky, called in to do a quick re-write, added a powerful humanist edge, he shows career cop Madigan (Richard Widmark) walking the tightrope between crime and law, considered crooked by his colleagues, suspected by the criminals (on whose goodwill he depends not only for extra income but also for information), but essentially a man of honour. The style has all Siegel's characteristic fury: cops dodging bullets as they move in on a besieged gunman, and Madigan's two-gun assault on the killer Benesch (Steve Inhat) in a poky apartment, terrifying in its unleashed brutality. Even interludes like the meeting with the dwarf gambling boss (Michael Dunn) on a deserted and windy beach promenade has a sexual overtone and suppressed violence that jump like a twitchy nerve. *Coogan's Bluff* (1968), comic but also more thoughtful, has Clint Eastwood's Coogan, an Arizonan lawman visiting New York to take custody of a fugitive, lose the man and hunt through the city to find him, a

*COOGAN'S BLUFF: Don Stroud, Tisha Sterling*

search that demonstrates the value of Madigan's flexible attitude to crime. Coogan's blind faith in frontier law and order is demolished by sociologist Susan Clark, whose attitude to criminals, even a delinquent who appreciatively fondles her breast, is one of detached sympathy, and by tough cop Lee J. Cobb, not afraid to make his contempt for Coogan's simplistic ethic devastatingly manifest ("Why are you doing this? Don't tell me. I know; there are some things a man's gotta do"). Coogan's education leads to the runaway's capture in Palisades Park after a motor-bike chase, and a fairer shake for the Indian renegade he tracks down on his return from his Eastern adventures, to whom he offers a conciliatory cigarette. The bloody demolition of a pool-room gang in a savage ballet of punches, kicks and cues wielded with deadly accuracy, and a furiously filmed attack at the airport when the fugitive couple (Don Stroud and Ann Sothern's daughter, Tisha Sterling) engineer an audacious escape, show Siegel's relish for violence, but the film's tone is as calm as Coogan himself, while some playful sexual interludes emphasise his belief that among the modern warriors there is time even for pleasure if ethics are not too rigidly observed. Cobb's "Relax. Let it happen" sums up the film's looseness and appeal.

Briton John Boorman directed *Point Blank* (1967) from a script by Alexander Jacobs, David and Rafe Newhouse from Richard Stark's "The Hunter" but its tone and the style of Lee Marvin as the juggernaut Walker owes much to Siegel's view of the urban world. A man's single-minded hunt for the wife and friend who betrayed him, leaving him for dead in the ruins of abandoned Alcatraz prison, becomes in Boorman's hands an exploration of the criminal power structure and an exposition of its brutal politics unsurpassed in action films of the post-war period. Walker tracks down and kills his friend Reese (John Vernon), sending him tumbling naked from a luxury penthouse, finds his wife (Sharon Acker) and causes her death, and eventually penetrates the centre of the criminal industry from which he hopes to extract his rightful gains, but in each case the victory is hollow: Reese doesn't have the money he stole, having used it to "buy into" the crime ring; his wife, abandoned by her lover and tormented by guilt, chooses to poison herself; and the top criminal (Carroll O'Connor) is a plump and nervous executive all of whose business happens on paper. Real money surfaces only once in the elaborate manipulations of the big-time, and that is in the midnight drop at Alcatraz, from which Walker is promised a cut if he will only collect it in person. A helicopter lands in the dark, deserted yard; the money is waiting, but Walker does not appear. At last

*POINT BLANK: Lee Marvin (left)*

he has understood, and the shadows of the old prison swallow him up. Siegel must have approved, but *Point Blank* goes further than Siegel, showing that the new criminal code must, if taken to its logical conclusion, supersede even basic human drives, offering a new sexuality of destruction to replace them. Bursting into his wife's house, Walker empties his pistol into the bed, slow-motion emphasising an orgasmic shudder that runs through his body as the gun discharges. Tempting the traitor Reese who hides surrounded by guards in a penthouse, he sends his sister-in-law (Angie Dickinson) to him, knowing that desire will make him careless, and although the girl shudders when touched by Reese, her sexual choreography is precisely, cunningly judged, as is her estimate of her appeal. "How badly does he want you?" Walker asks, and the girl, on consideration, says "Pretty bad." Love and remorse have no place in a world built on power, as the girl at last realises when, despairing of ever attracting the attention of the phlegmatic Walker, whom she has come to love, she attacks

*Julie Harris, Jim Brown, Warren Oates and Donald Sutherland in*
*THE SPLIT*

him as a mechanism, turning on all the electrical appliances in the gang-leader's villa, then throwing herself at him with a fusillade of blows that leaves her exhausted and him, for the first time, both physically dazed and sexually excited. "This guy's beautiful," the professional gunman says to his employer after Walker has destroyed one of their top men, "he's tearing you to pieces," a phrase distilling the essence of this love affair with force.

Marvin continued a distinguished career with a precise and animalistic portrayal of the American soldier in Boorman's existential parable of war, *Hell in the Pacific* (1969), and after an unaccountable singing (or croaking) role in Joshua Logan's *Paint Your Wagon* (1969) — a projected musical remake of *The African Queen* with Marvin and Doris Day thankfully never eventuated — played an ageing cowboy in *Monte Walsh* (1970), a self-indulgent but moving directorial debut by William Fraker, cameraman on the Logan film and many of the Sixties most effective productions. He was also to have starred in Gordon Flemyng's *The Split* (1968) but abdicated to Jim Brown, ex-football hero and one of the few black actors to challenge Sidney Poitier's position as Hollywood's Negro conscience. Based on another Richard Stark novel, "The Seventh," and very similar to *Point Blank* even to having a hero known only by his surname (in this case McClain), *The Split*, like Boorman's film, passed over the crime, a stadium robbery during a football match, in favour of analysing how the gang was formed and the loot divided, an echo of Kubrick's historic *The Killing*. McClain's recruitment of the team, including sharply tense scenes for Warren Oates and the elegant Donald Sutherland, the meaningless death of Ellie (Diahann Carroll) that throws the plan awry, an unpleasant torture scene in a slippery steam bath, and the final shot of McClain pausing during his get-away at the imagined sound of the dead Ellie calling his name, all show a keen intelligence. The sense of a new school of thrillers persists as one pursues *Point Blank*'s influence. Quincy Jones, whose soul-oriented score for *The Split* gave bite to the film, also composed the music for *In the Heat of the Night* (Norman Jewison, 1967) in which Sidney Poitier tackled the problems that Siegel, Boorman and Flemyng had dealt with. A runaway box-office success, this film and its central character, urbane Northern Negro detective Virgil Tibbs, were too slight to justify their enormous reputation. When Rod Steiger as the seedy Southern police chief fails to cow Tibbs, and is lured instead into confessing his own loneliness and despair, the one-dimensional conflict of black against white has been exhausted. A rural detective story remains, with Poitier's forensic skill and education pitted against the problem of a murdered businessman in a small town and the hunt for his killer. Only fine supporting performances from Warren Oates as a sly deputy and Lee Grant as the widow rise above Jewison's slickly professional direction, though photography of bruised

blues and dusty yellows from Haskell Wexler make the film never less than delightful to watch.

As unlikely a lawman as Poitier, Frank Sinatra took a hand at underworld films, mostly under the director Gordon Douglas, who also handled the unsatisfactory sequel to *In the Heat of the Night*, *They Call Me Mister Tibbs* (1970). In *Ocean's 11* (1960), a routine "big caper" comedy-thriller with Sinatra an unconvincing mastermind, Lewis Milestone took charge, and Jack Donohue for *Assault on a Queen* (1966), about the attempted hijack of the "Queen Mary" with a refloated wartime submarine. Douglas returned as director for two Miami-based private-eye films, *Tony Rome* (1967) and *Lady in Cement* (1968). Unlike Dean Martin, Sinatra is a singer whose acting talents are not easily written off. Correctly handled, his well-timed delivery and "lived-in" face can add much to a film, but not all his Sixties productions capitalised on this. *Tony Rome*, set like *Gunn* in the homosexual underworld, and the more comic *Lady in Cement* shared a wisecracking energy, despite the latter's grotesque casting: Martin Gabel, perhaps the only actor in Hollywood shorter than Sinatra, played a gang leader, and Raquel Welch his girl. The sight of Sinatra, his face like an old tennis shoe, romancing the sex symbol of the decade is one over which all his admirers prefer to draw a veil, though it makes all the more surprising the collaboration of Douglas and Sinatra on *The Detective* (1968), a shadowed and relentless picture of New York's dirty underside, with Sinatra a cop trying to unravel, despite the demands of a nymphomaniac wife (a role written for Mia Farrow but played with great subtlety by Lee Remick), the murder of a rich homosexual. His search, though lacking the cynical depth of Siegel, has notable moments: homosexuals urged, cowering and terrified, out of their meeting place, a parked furniture van, into the blue-white light of police torches; Sinatra moving around the apartment of the murdered man, describing unemotionally the details of a corpse's mutilation; an edgy and cleanly played argument with crooked cop Ralph Meeker.

Among the new thrillers, the work of Samuel Fuller had become slightly *passé*, his pre-Cinemascope intimacy of style superseded by Siegel's whirling vitality, but in choice of subjects he remained uniquely individual and provocative. His comments on war in *Verboten!* (1960), a talkative examination of neo-Nazism in Germany opening with a remarkable

*Sidney Poitier: IN THE HEAT OF THE NIGHT*

*Mutilation murder. Frank Sinatra in* THE DETECTIVE

sequence of Allied soldiers crashing through the rubble of Berlin to Beethoven's Fifth, and in *Merrill's Marauders* (1962), a highly-coloured jungle action story that disguised its moral force and concise picture of war's psychological effects under a lively surface, with Jeff Chandler memorable as the indestructible Merrill, are as fresh as anything in the Sixties. *Shock Corridor* (1963), banned in many countries because of the attack on conditions in mental hospitals contained in the story of a reporter feigning insanity to carry out his investigation, and *The Naked Kiss* (1964), his parable of good and evil in a small town where a retired prostitute (Constance Towers) shows herself more virtuous than even the noblest of her critics, displayed marked contrasts in style — the first harshly violent, the second silky in its Stanley Cortez photography and elegant playing — but an impatience with the bland morality of the Fifties unites them, relating to Siegel's attacks on the same hypocrisy. *The Naked Kiss*, opening with an indelible image of the whore attacking and robbing the pimp who has shaved her head as a punishment, shows Fuller's extraordinary vision at its most corrosive, but his ethic has its least guarded expression in *Underworld USA* (1961), dealing with Cliff Robertson's search for his father's murderers that leads him to use and destroy all those he meets, even the woman who loves him. A classic scene has him offering the only bribe of any value to a dying witness, forgiveness, in return for the killers' names. These given, Robertson rejects the man's plea for absolution with a callous "Sucker," the one word conveying a terrifying nihilism.

Also emphasising the dichotomy between society and the realities of power, *Cape Fear* (J. Lee Thompson, 1962) faced attorney Gregory Peck with total violence in the person of criminal Robert Mitchum, who returns to a small town, making no secret of the fact that he proposes to revenge himself on Peck, his wife and family, for sending him to jail. Mitchum waits his chance as Peck tries to urge his friends and the law into action, an impossible task since Mitchum has, as yet, committed no crime. The issues are

*THE NAKED KISS: Constance Towers*

*BULLITT: Steve McQueen and George S. Brown*

those of the Siegel films, the villain's playing as horrific in its lazy menace as Marvin's and the *dénouement* in the swamps gratuitously sadistic. Not a fragrant story, *Cape Fear* courageously faces the issue, postulating the only reasonable answer, a reliance on personal force. The same themes appear veiled in Martin Ritt's *The Brotherhood* (1968), where an American Mafia clan readjusts to the organisation's new status as a semi-legitimate business. Alex Cord is the new man, an accountant with little taste for killing, and Kirk Douglas his older brother in whom the rituals of murder and retribution are ingrained. Discovering for the first time which Mafia elders were involved in his father's murder, Douglas urges Cord into a pact of revenge, and when the younger man refuses, embarks on a personal vendetta that ends only when Cord is required by the council to shoot him down. Ritt gives us a different view of New York — discoloured, untidy — while his carefully chosen supporting cast redeems lapses into superficial "colour" like the scenes of family celebration: Murray Hamilton as a terse Mafia executive; Luther Adler, the fat, terrified killer whom Douglas makes his first victim, ramming a gun barrel into his belly as they laugh over the details of a half-forgotten murder, and later letting him slowly strangle to death; Eduardo Cianelli, most durable of Hollywood henchmen, as a riven-faced and skeletal don entrusting to Douglas responsibility for the blood feud.

The task of compounding the new crime film's conflicting elements and making the most assured statement of its ethic was left to English director Peter Yates who in *Bullitt* (1968) created a thriller precisely characteristic of Hollywood in the Sixties. A straightforward if eccentrically-told account of a gang skirmish, with San Francisco cop Bullitt (Steve McQueen), a dead Grand Jury witness on his hands, unravelling the details of his death and its significance before being demoted by a politically ambitious District Attorney (Robert Vaughn), nothing in the plot suggests the film's excitement, which springs, as in *Bloody Mama* and *Bonnie and Clyde*, from a

*BULLITT: Steve McQueen, Pat Renella*

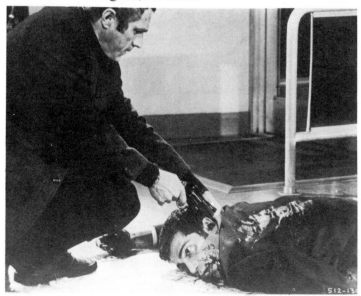

sophisticated manipulation of violence. Action erupts out of quietness: the snick of a safety belt signalling the start of a vertiginous car chase around the hills of San Francisco; the gunmen's car closing in and blasting Bullitt's with a shot-gun while both race along the sunny freeway; bystanders throwing themselves in a wave to the ground as the cop draws a bead on his quarry at the airport. Unlike *Madigan, Bullitt* does not emphasise philosophy or motivation, except in brief scenes where Bullitt's girl, Jacqueline Bisset, voices the brutality of his life, and he, after killing his man, returns home to wash his hands in a last enigmatic shot. Siegel's postulation has become Yates's way of life. The suave DA runs with the aristocracy, unconcerned with the issues of social justice central to serious crime films of other decades; even the criticisms of public indifference and political manipulation present in Robert L. Pike's original novel "Mute Witness," have been removed by scenarists Alan R. Trustman and Harry Kleiner, along with Pike's unheroic and ageing detective. Bullitt lives comfortably, attended by a smart *équipe,* takes his pleasures as a right, and with little reference to those who provide them. At the hospital, when a nurse with a lunch tray, seeing Bullitt, asks "Are you the policeman who hasn't had anything to eat?", he gratefully grabs the tray and disappears munching, as the uniformed guard, for whom the meal was intended, stares stoically ahead, unable to complain. One senses that the civilization where everybody wears a gun can boast, like the Western frontier of the 1880s, a harmony and singleness of purpose our own unbalanced world has never known. *Bullitt, Madigan* and *Point Blank* argue for a suspension of the rules that restrain us from total violence, while persuasively stressing the beauty and excitement of this anarchic world and the logic connoted by Harper's "cream and bastards" apophthegm. As social beings we may be repelled, but the euphoria these films engender suggests that they are only telling us things we already unconsciously know.

# 7. The Perfumed Battlefield

SINCE 1909, when D. W. Griffith hired Mary Pickford for a series of Biograph one-reelers in which two hopeful suitors competed for her demure favours undeterred by her playing of one off against the other, the sex comedy has been a staple of American cinema, hanging on tenaciously even in the Sixties. With *Pillow Talk* (Michael Gordon, 1958) Universal producer Ross Hunter began a series of films in which Doris Day's career-girl designer, advertising executive or businesswoman was pitted against the decade's symbol of heterosexual virility, Rock Hudson, a contest that involved Hudson in frequent sexual humiliation but ended with the couple in each other's arms. Doris Day's perky persona, all pill-box hats and boyish collars, had proven box-official appeal, and the failure of *Midnight Lace* (David Miller, 1960), a copy of *Gaslight* in which she played a rich wife being badgered out of her mind by suave husband Rex Harrison, showed that the public preferred the Doris they knew. Resolutely ignoring the wrinkles (when a producer mentioned them, Doris Day told him the cameraman was getting old, not her; in fact when she made *Midnight Lace* she confessed to being thirty-six) and guided by her astute husband Marty Melcher, she persisted with Hunter/Hudson farces. The self-satisfied Hudson, whose major strength as an actor is his ability to convey in the same expression arrogance and the petulance of a slapped child, was born to have his vanity punctured and Day to puncture it. By degrees, the Day character became more assured and Hudson evolved into the ultimate "Playboy" male, seducing with the weary calculation of a big-game hunter while less well-endowed friends looked admiringly on. His reference in *A Very Special Favor* (Michael Gordon, 1965) to his bedroom as "the perfumed battlefield" clarified the relationship of these cynical comedies to the amoral crime films, defining sex as just another device in the code of combat.

In all these films, Hudson (or Kirk Douglas, or Cary Grant) is a rich bachelor famous for his appeal to women. In the overlong and unfunny *A Very Special Favor* they compete to cook his breakfast, do his washing and clean his apartment for no more reward than Hudson's babyish smile. As an attorney he even wins a case in France by seducing the female judge, encouraging Charles Boyer, who lost the suit, to approach him in the capacity of consultant to seduce his daughter (Leslie Caron), a career psychoanalyst of whose future sexual happiness he is in doubt. Such bland amorality would have made production unthinkable ten years before, but a stream of Day/Hudson sexual duels had made it merely *risqué*. Recognising that such heights might outdistance the average viewer, most of the films give the Hudson/Grant/Douglas character an ineffectual assistant whose duty it is to mope admiringly in the corner and suffer by proxy for the excesses of his friend, a role talented comedian Gig Young made into a useful meal-ticket. In *For Love or Money* (Michael Gordon, 1963) he is stranded naked on a pole in the middle of a fog-bound harbour as his mentor, attorney Kirk Douglas, sails away with heiress Mitzi Gaynor, while in *Strange Bedfellows* (Melvin Frank, 1965) he plays a company lawyer trying to stabilise the marriage of oil-man Hudson and revolutionist Gina Lollobrigida and thus make him acceptable to the board as a potential executive. Like most good actors, Young responded to superior material. He was the wistful academic assistant to tycoon Cary Grant in Delbert Mann's highly profitable ($8.5 million gross) *That Touch of Mink* (1962), acting as his emissary in the pursuit of office girl Doris Day, and suffering the indignities meted out by her protective friend, automat waitress Joyce Meadows, who has pegged Young as a potential seducer. His polite approach to the automat windows rewarded by a dessert in the face from her invisible hand is the cleverest of modern pie-throwing gags, and his pleas for Grant to stop raising his salary so that he can retreat to Harvard and the scholar's life gave coherence to an otherwise wandering film. Grant's playing suggests the weakness of the Hudson/Day formula; the cringing Rock might well be afflicted on his wedding night by a rash brought on through fear of marriage, but an assertive Grant in this situation does not convince.

As usual, one film in the flood of carbon copies dominates its lacklustre neighbours. *Lover Come Back* (Delbert Mann, 1962), thanks to a deft Stanley Shapiro/Paul Henning script, juggles the elements cleverly, extracting from Day and Hudson their best performances. Tony Randall, the inept straight man, is introduced marvellously when he strides, wielding a cane, into the office of Hudson, business manager of the family advertising firm, and berates him for an excess of independence, until Hudson abstractedly breaks the stick over his knee, reducing Randall to blubbering recriminations. Competing with Day's firm for a big account, Hudson steals it with an all-night orgy for the Southern sponsor. His rival discovers the man (veteran comic Jack Oakie) alone in the disordered apartment at

*LOVER COME BACK: Jack Oakie, Edie Adams, Rock Hudson.*

dawn, blissfully plucking an abandoned bass fiddle and murmuring, "Now ah've seen *every*thang." Hudson's cool finally cracks when Randall, in a fit of piqued independence, issues some commercials for a fictitious product called "Vip" produced as a bribe to make chorus girl Rebel Davis (Edie Adams) testify on his behalf at an Advertising Council hearing. Eccentric scientist Jack Kruschen agrees to invent "Vip" to answer the resulting nation-wide demand, and after a series of multi-coloured explosions in his basement laboratory produces it — a mint that turns to pure alcohol in the blood. "Just what this country needs," he bellows as the Advertising Council munches itself insensible; "a good ten-cent drunk."

To everybody's surprise, Howard Hawks also entered the field with *Man's Favorite Sport?* (1964), a curiosity he may have since regretted producing. When the script, by John Fenton Murray and Steve McNeil, proved unsatisfactory, Hawks's regular writer Leigh Brackett reworked it,

*MAN'S FAVORITE SPORT?: Rock Hudson, Maria Perschy*

inserting, with Hawks's collusion, an anthology of gags borrowed from vintage comedies, including the elaborate battle with a fish from *Libeled Lady* (1936) directed by his crony Jack Conway. Mixing Hawksian sexual warfare with the bland traditions of the Ross Hunter comedy, the film has Hudson playing Abercrombie and Fitch's expert on fly-fishing who has gained all his knowledge from books. Lured by Paula Prentiss and her friend Maria Perschy to Lake Wakapoogee Lodge for their fishing competition, he must demonstrate a non-existent ability to his boss John McGiver. Relying on sight-gags more worthy of Jerry Lewis — chased by a bear, Hudson runs across the surface of the water before slowly sinking, and later is whisked across the lake by a pair of inflatable waders — the film lacks Hawks's usual crackling sexual tensions, though the relationship between aggressive Prentiss and meek Hudson occasionally rises to the level of *Bringing up Baby*'s duller moments.

Various studios pursued different variations on the "Playboy" philosophy and middle-aged character comedians were never short of work. In *Under the Yum Yum Tree* (David Swift, 1963) Jack Lemmon played a classic wish-fulfilment figure, the bachelor landlord who rents his apartments only to nubile young women, filling his own pad with an awesome variety of aids to seduction. Based on a stage success, the film exploits the techniques of French farce and has occasional coy flashes of sex, acting honors being stolen by Paul Lynde as Lemmon's randy gardener, shivering deliciously at the thought of his boss's nightly exertions, greeting him with an admiring "Hiya, hot shot" and reassuring him, as a "Playboy" reader to somebody who actually lives it, "You're OK with *me*, big boy." Less effectively, Lemmon was a bachelor strip-cartoonist in *How to Murder Your Wife* (Richard Quine, 1965), living out the fantasies of his sub-Bond hero until hooked by the attractive Virna Lisi, and in *Come Blow Your Horn* (Bud Yorkin, 1963) Frank Sinatra repeated his role in *The Tender Trap* as a hyper-potent playboy, this time initiating his younger brother into the arts of high living until, rather surprisingly, its emptiness dawns on him, and he abandons hedonism for marriage. Tony Bill as the brother and Lee J. Cobb as the father nicely convey a combination of awe and admiration for Sinatra's riotous existence, Bill visibly falling in love with dissipation when he arrives in the aftermath of a party, unrolling the collapsible bed to find a befuddled guest, complete with trombone, inside, and watching another victim, a half-gallon can of tomato juice under his arm, pull back the blind, only to recoil with a hoarse cry of agony from the light. *Boys' Night Out* (Michael Gordon, 1962) takes a less jaundiced view of amoral luxury, with a group of husbands, including Tony Randall and bachelor James Garner, subscribing to a fund with which they rent a flat and install Kim Novak, a collective mistress whose favours they are afraid to sample — happily, since she is a sociology student using the situation as a case study in sexual attitudes. Again, the supporting cast saves a stodgy and excessively coy plot: Jim Backus, showing the doubtful clients over his apartment, gives them both barrels, silently indicating a bronze mirror covering the bedroom ceiling and, when Randall, with cold feet, attempts to back out because the flat has no wine rack, reveals an enormous fixture behind a sliding panel with a contemptuous "No wine rack? Who do you think we let this place to — savages?"

Given a Hollywood obsession with the mechanics of seduction, it was inevitable that some studios would turn to the quasi-sociological manuals

*HOW TO MURDER YOUR WIFE: Jack Lemmon, Virna Lisi*

*BOY'S NIGHT OUT: Tony Randall, Howard Duff, James Garner*

of sexual combat popular during the tentatively permissive mid-Sixties. Novelist Joseph Heller, hot property since the success of his book "Catch--22," was hired, with Daniel R. Schwartz, to create a script from Helen Gurley Brown's *Sex and the Single Girl* (Richard Quine, 1965), a factual description of male seduction methods and how gracefully to accept or reject them. The film emerged as a variation on the Hudson/Day formula with Natalie Wood as Helen Brown, a doctor of sex, eluding and encouraging muck-raking journalist Tony Curtis with the techniques outlined in her book; even devotees could find little of Heller in the predictable dialogue. More effectively, Gene Kelly's funny and highly profitable *A Guide for the Married Man* (1967) offered useful tips for the bored husband as Robert Morse introduced eager Walter Matthau to the techniques of suburban infidelity. Some were grotesque — by using garlic salad dressing as after-shave lotion, Matthau leads his wife to purchase the "Old Gunpowder" deodorant that will cover the perfume of any other woman — but many had

95

the ring of authenticity, as had Morse's exposition of them as he and Matthau went about the dread routine of life in a suburban matriarchal society, a tribute to Kelly's imaginative direction and Frank Tarloff's ingenious script, from his own book.

Also related to sexual documentary, Bud Yorkin's *Divorce American Style* (1967) belies its flippant advertising and clean-cut stars (Dick Van Dyke, Debbie Reynolds) with an acid picture of the divorce culture and its ludicrous traditions. Reynolds and Van Dyke, bickering suburbanites, are whisked towards divorce by others used to seeing marriages break up and only too willing to help out. The joint bank account is looted by a doubtful Reynolds at the insistence of her "practical" friend, lawyers called in who, chatting amiably about mutual cronies, carve up the estate with all but the scraps going to the wife. "The house to you, the mortgage to me," Van Dyke rages. "You get the uranium mine; I get the shaft." In the aftermath, Yorkin explores the glum society of the divorced. Reynolds is involved with a group of the re-married (and re-divorced) the parentage of whose children only insider Tom Bosley can unravel, while Van Dyke, chugging around town in his decrepit Volkswagen, finds that, among divorcees who remain single, the problems are greater. Destitute Jason Robards has the sympathy of his wife, who lives in comfort on his alimony, but the only legal way to restore her ex-husband's solvency is to remarry, an end towards which he works by acting as marriage broker. The obligatory happy ending — Reynolds under hypnosis at a night-club performing an improvised strip-tease for Van Dyke (no actress since Mary Pickford has shown Debbie Reynold's anxiety to destroy her girl-next-door image — compromises the story, but its edge returns when, with the two remarried, the eternal bickering breaks out once more.

Hollywood's Sixties reliance on such complex comedy forms conflicted with its lack of young and attractive stars skilled in comic timing. Day, Hudson, Grant and Sinatra gradually lost conviction as sex symbols, and no younger star was even remotely able to handle the precise mechanics of comedy. A partial exception, Cliff Robertson in *Sunday in New York* (1964), working with a Norman Krasna script, outacted both Jane Fonda and Rod Taylor as the girl-hunting airline pilot who arrives at his New York *pied-à-terre* to find Taylor in the process of seducing his sister. His politely sceptical receipt of Taylor's explanation and the would-be lovers' growing confusion in the face of it lift the film briefly to the level of classic bedroom farce. Krasna's lifetime of comic experience shows itself in continuing gags like Robertson's rendezvous with air hostess Jo Morrow, constantly delayed when their planes fail to land on schedule, leaving her stranded in a distant city wailing "Where *are* you?" on the long-distance telephone, more dishevelled and desperate with each call. Without such accomplished *farceurs* as Robertson (who revealed hidden talent in 1969 with *Charly* (Ralph Nelson), the story of an idiot restored to full intelligence before sliding once again into mindlessness, which Robertson courageously produced, winning himself an acting Oscar) the sex comedy could deteriorate into lamely cast romps where humour took second place to lush presentation, typified by *If a Man Answers* (Henry Levin, 1962) in which Bobby Darin as an unlikely fashion photographer sets his cap for the un-appetising Sandra Dee. The same couple provided light relief in *Come September* (Robert Mulligan, 1961), overshadowed by Rock Hudson and Gina Lollobrigida as tycoon and mistress who restrict themselves to one glorious September meeting in an Italian villa each year, a plot that even the talented Mulligan could bring only fitfully to life.

Occasional delights came from veterans whose skill obscured the faults of story, not to mention the crude innuendo of a script. *Yours, Mine and Ours* (Melville Shavelson, 1968) cast Henry Fonda and Lucille Ball as widower and widow who marry, achieving a collective family of eighteen. The marriage's problems, psychological and logistical, are amusingly shown, not only from the parents' point of view but also that of the children. In a delightful sequence, Navy officer Fonda's service system for efficient home life is seen by the youngest boy: beginning with his glum statement, "My job was to clean my teeth, and let me tell you it wasn't easy," he is shown crowded out of the bathroom by larger siblings, deprived in the same way of breakfast and his own overshoes, and in the last shot clumps to school in enormous boots with the resigned comment, "There was nothing else for it. I was forced to invent the oatmeal sand-wich." The film's best line comes from Tom Bosley as a doctor called in the middle of a thunderstorm as the integration of the two families is at its most hectic. Seeing masses of screaming children race by in the gloom, he asks diffidently, "What did you say your institution was called?"

Cary Grant continued a comedy career of phenomenal consistency. Stanley Donen's *The Grass is Greener* (1960), less than sparkling despite its attractive English stately home setting (even Donen called the film "too slow") would have died without Grant as the aristocratic husband urged into protectiveness by a genteel romance between his wife (Deborah Kerr) and American millionaire tourist Robert Mitchum. His puzzled pique mixed with British reserve gives even the feeblest jokes a witty edge, and one can easily forget, watching his casual playing, how precise a technician he is. Engaging in a slightly drunken duel with Mitchum, he arranges to be shot in the arm, and engagingly sends up the stereotyped stiff-upper-lip victim, while in *Father Goose* (Ralph Nelson, 1965) his handling of an Oscar-winning Peter Stone/Frank Tarloff script gives to the promising situation, of a boozy coast-watcher trapped on a Japanese-occupied island with Leslie Caron and her class of fugitive schoolgirls, new dimensions both of pathos and comedy. Stand-bys like the Slow Dawning and the Double Take are given new life in his hands. When Caron imagines herself bitten by a snake, Grant, on advice from base that recovery is unlikely, plays the traditional death scene, plying the girl with whisky to ease the pain, making her comfortable, listening to her ramblings (caused by the whisky) and sadly drawing the sheet over her face as she loses consciousness, dead drunk. A child brings in the stick Caron mistook for a snake, and tries to explain what happened. Grant holds it at arm's length and stares at it, saying accusingly, "*That's* not a snake." Long pause. "It *looks* like a snake" — pause — "but it isn't". Some time after, light dawns.

Beyond the sex war and its parables of seduction, the comedy romance had little scope, and it was left to Europeans to make the stories of romantic love — *Un Homme et une Femme* (Claude Lelouch, 1967), *Far From the Madding Crowd* (John Schlesinger, 1967), *Doctor Zhivago* (David Lean, 1966) — that sustained this form in world cinema. Preoccupied with sexual documentary, American producers seemed to have lost the knack, though in *Breakfast at Tiffany's* (1961) Blake Edwards and scenarist George Axelrod achieved a sweetened version of Truman Capote's fanciful novelette about a dizzily amoral New York sprite who floats above the squalid realities of city life. Audrey Hepburn, one of the few actresses capable of realising the part of Holly Golightly, falsifies the original's despair, but her characterisation is charming. Edwards pushes the story's romance beyond its capacity, and though Patricia Neal shows her usual dry authority as the rich patron to George Peppard's struggling writer, the cast is unable, especially in scenes like the final search in the rain for a lost pet, to square Capote's cynicism with Edwards's sugary approach. Yet images of Peppard in the autumnal park talking about Holly and her past with her ex-husband, a stiff and ageing Ozark farmer (Buddy Ebsen), or Holly in the opening sequence munching doughnuts on the ledge of Tiffany's window in the

*Walter Matthau and Jack Lemmon: THE ODD COUPLE*

pre-dawn gloom are defiantly memorable. Adapted like most of the decade's screen romances from a successful play, Neil Simon's *Barefoot in the Park* (Gene Saks, 1967), a series of incidents in the life of New York newly-weds Jane Fonda and Robert Redford, enjoyed immense commerical success. Sexually charming, Fonda and Redford were outclassed by the supporting cast, including Mildred Natwick as Fonda's mother, progressively more breathless on each arrival at their top-floor flat. Finding that the husband has left home after a tiff, she is berated by her daughter for not stopping him. "What do you think he was carrying a suitcase for?" "Knowing how neat he is," Natwick says reflectively, "I thought — the garbage?" Saks and Simon followed this success with *The Odd Couple* (1968), a further exploration of domestic life in the story of two middle-aged divorcees (Walter Matthau and Jack Lemon) who share an apartment. Effective on stage, the story suffers, as some musicals had, from expansion

to another medium, and although no film with such actors could fail to be funny, abrasive playing does not always sustain the attenuated material.

A romance commendably free of sentiment, *Two for the Road* (1967) leads Hollywood's Sixties fantasies on the problems of marriage. Shot in England and France by Stanley Donen from a screenplay by English novelist Frederic Raphael (scenarist also of John Schlesinger's *Far from the Madding Crowd* and *Darling*), the film concisely summarises the complex mechanics of a relationship. As Donen follows Audrey Hepburn and Albert Finney through meeting, love and courtship, and then their subsequent marriage's decline and revival, Raphael's obvious understanding of the couple involves us totally in their story. Taking as a basis the road journey from London to the South of France, he compares the occasions on which they have made this trip, contrasting incidents from various stages in their lives to show that love metamorphoses, but that at last, after misunderstandings and infidelities, a new basis for affection emerges, more satisfying than youthful passion or middle-aged indifference, the higher state of marriage John Updike so perceptively analysed in "Couples." Christopher Challis's photography with its glowing fields of yellow, dusty blue skies and hard colours of the Côte d'Azur, conveys perfectly the sense of a landscape reflecting emotional states, while Raphael scores shrewdly on French idiosyncracies, contrasting them with the occasionally brutal British sense of the absurd. Dining *al fresco* with rich friends, Finney, asked by his hostess to ring for the maid, presses by mistake the button that collapses the awning. As its folds descend around them, his muffled voice is heard saying, "That's the trouble with this part of the world. You don't get much of a sunset."

It was the essence of the Hudson/Day comedies that a sexual combat existed between man and woman, and that each side desired this to be the case. They would not have achieved even their meagre level of humour had audiences not recognised in the story feelings and actions they had experienced themselves. A few films, by contrast, acknowledged the rules but, instead of setting their action within them, made them the subject of brutal parody. Billy Wilder, whose acid style as a scriptwriter and director had corroded most emotional conventions, found Sixties sexual *mores* ludicrous, and attacked them with fury and relish. *The Apartment* (1960) satirised boy-meets-girl, with minor office worker Jack Lemmon lending

*TWO FOR THE ROAD: Audrey Hepburn*

his apartment to superiors for their after-office affairs in the hope of promotion, and seeing his own secret love, round-heeled elevator operator Shirley MacLaine, taken there by executive Fred MacMurray; they meet only when the girl attempts suicide in his apartment and Lemmon saves her life. Lemmon's deference to his superiors, the weary consultation of his diary to decide whether yet another randy colleague can be accommodated, the regimented corps of account clerks clacking rhythmically on their adding machines sum up the meaninglessness of this dehumanised city life, mocking Lemmon's ambition just as his act of sadly plucking a string of spaghetti from the tennis racquet used to strain it when MacLaine was his dinner guest mocks all melancholy romanticism.

Wilder's remaining projects of the Sixties, all, like *The Apartment,* with scripts by his regular collaborator I. A. L. Diamond, show a similar cynicism. Margaret Monnot's musical *Irma la Douce* (1963) was stripped

*IRMA LA DOUCE: Shirley MacLaine*

of its songs to become a vehicle for Shirley MacLaine as the Parisian whore with a heart of gold and Jack Lemmon as the cop who loves her, roles that repeated most of the themes, but with less impact, of *The Apartment. One Two Three* (1961) ostensibly parodied the Cold War and dollar imperialism, and less obviously the traditions of whirlwind romance, James Cagney playing with appalling vigour Coca-Cola's Berlin manager who desperately unsnarls the affair of the chairman's daughter (Pamela Tiffin) with Communist Horst Buchholz. Wilder uses his middle-European background to home in on German regimentation and the grim gaiety of East German high life. Wooing Cagney, a potential source of graft, three commissars ply him with champagne, offer him the latest Zim automobile ("Is genuine copy of 1947 Nash") and, as the superannuated band thumps out "Yes, We Have No Bananas," bellow, "Vaiter, more visky. Kapellmeister, more rock und roll." In *The Fortune Cookie* (1966) *(Meet Whiplash Willie* in U.K.),Wilder again exploited Jack Lemmon as the poor sap, in this case a television cameraman whose spectacular accident while shooting a football match makes him the meat of his attorney brother-in-law "Whiplash Willie" (Walter Matthau) who puts him in a plaster cast and claims extortionate damages for injury. New responsibilities crowd in on the hapless victim; his greedy wife (Judi West) returns to bolster the illusion of domestic bliss and take her cut, the player (Ron Rich) who believes himself responsible for Lemmon's injuries is racked with suicidal despair, and over the street detectives set up cameras in the hope of catching him out. Humour is subordinated to satire, and Lemmon edged into the position of an upside-down hero of our time, asserting himself at last in favour of poverty, loneliness and illusion; as in most of Wilder's films, one instinctively prefers the villain.

Of all Wilder's parodies, *Kiss Me, Stupid* (1964) is both the funniest and most accurate, so cheerfully flagrant in its amorality that Hollywood erupted in horror and the American Legion of Decency awarded it a "Condemned" rating. In Diamond's adaptation of an obscure Italian farce, Ray Walston and Cliff Osmond, amateur composers in the town of Climax, Nevada, sabotage the car of singer Dean Martin, stranding him in town overnight and hoping during that time to interest him in their songs. Knowing Martin's appetite for women (without what he calls "*action* action" every night, Dino wakes up with a terrible headache) the hysterically jealous Walston gets his dumb wife (Felicia Farr) out of town for the night and hires to impersonate her the town whore, "Polly the Pistol" (Kim

Novak), waitress at "The Belly Button," a roadside bar outside town where, "recommended by the bar-tender," she struggles to accumulate enough money to leave Climax. Parodying his own image of the lecherous drunk, Martin revels in his good fortune as Walston urges him to make love to his "wife" and the couple ply him with liquor. "Why does your husband call you 'lamb chop'?" he asks Novak; she murmurs, "Maybe it's because I wear paper panties," and Martin sinks to the floor at the orgy's height muttering "Paper panties, paper panties." When Farr returns unexpectedly and, thinking that Walston rather than a stranger is in the shower, reaches in passing through the curtain and playfully slaps him on the rump, the delight and puzzlement on Martin's face as it emerges from the steam, like his glassy disbelief (and Novak's ) as Walston performs one of his songs, "I'm a Poached Egg," shows the singer's gamy talent at its best.

The point of Wilder's fable emerges at the conclusion, Walston increasingly drawn to and protective of Polly, and she slipping comfortably into the role of wife and mother, while Farr, sullenly nursing her irritation at "The Belly Button," drinks herself into a stupour and is put to sleep in Polly's trailer. When the puzzled and frustrated Martin is ordered out of the house by Walston's sudden burst of rectitude over his fake wife, he finds his way to the bar and, on being directed to Polly's caravan, makes love to the complaisant Farr, who extracts from him a hefty fee and a promise to use Walston's song on his show — "The big ones are always the nicest," its astonished composers conclude when they hear it performed. To placate the censors, Wilder reshot the scene between Martin and Farr, showing him falling asleep before the commencement of "*action* action," but there is no doubt as to how the incident was meant to end, just as Farr patting Martin's behind in the shower merely cleans up a story that has become part of the mythology of embarrassing moments. Peter Sellers, who started in Walston's role but had a heart attack after a few weeks, would have given *Kiss Me, Stupid* a comic subtlety it lacks, but Walston's stringy assurance obviously fits Wilder's concept of the emasculated American male, of whom Lemmon's sniffling, feeble office worker in *The Apartment* is the archetype.

# 8. Go West

AMONG HOLLYWOOD *genres*, only the Western resisted an inflation of style and theme. Bigger and more expensive mainly in their star line-ups, most Westerns respected the rival traditions established by Budd Boetticher and John Sturges in the Fifties, and producers attempting epic Westerns, notably Cinerama's *How the West Was Won* (1962), found, since landscape and history imposed a leisurely and undramatic form, that the result lacked conviction. Essential elements like the desert and the journey could be given epic quality only by assigning symbolic values (the basis of John Ford's work), not by the mere addition of melodrama. As the producers of *Mackenna's Gold* (J. Lee Thompson, 1969) discovered, a valley whose hidden entrance and golden walls might enliven a Hercules historical drama fell flat as the object of a desert trek by cowboys. *The Way West* (Andrew V. McLaglen, 1967) and *The Hallelujah Trail* (John Sturges, 1965) failed in a spectacular approach to wagon trains and frontier settlement, though the latter, with whisky runners attempting to bring liquor to a resolutely "dry" Denver, had comic energy. Portions of *The Alamo* (1960), directed with surprising aplomb by John Wayne (John Ford helped briefly, but his footage was never used), combined spectacle with a feeling for character, capturing the mythological force of Davy Crockett and Sam Houston. Despite a style recalling the tableaux of DeMille, *The Alamo* shows visual flair, and a realisation that, in this field, old ideas are best. Hawksian night sequences set half-lit figures against a steely blackness, and a shot of Wayne's Crockett and his mountain boys riding through waist-high grass from which startled birds erupt evokes an untouched, uncorrupted world of legendary heroes.

Among big-budget Westerns, the prize for prodigality went to Marlon Brando's *One Eyed Jacks* (1961). Started by Stanley Kubrick, who left after disputes with the star, this film cost millions before the addition of Brando's huge fee, which included a large share of the gross and eventual ownership of the negative. Delays because of his insistence that actors improvise (rewards of up to $300 were offered to extras, out of Brando's own pocket, for the most effective reactions in key scenes like the hero's flogging and mutilation), and his insistence on "perfect" waves in the sea-coast sequences that kept the crew waiting for weeks (at $50,000 a day) made *One Eyed Jacks* a commercial disaster, yet the film has undoubted

artistic merit. Brando sees landscape with a fresh eye; the cliffs and narrow beaches of Monterey, and the bald, dusty desert hills are shot in Vista-Vision with genius by cameraman Charles Lang Jnr., making this one of the most beautiful Westerns ever produced. Brando's search for Karl Malden's symbolically-named "Dad" Longworth, an old confederate who, after abandoning his friend, turned to the law, becomes a saga of revenge and retribution with few precedents, compromised only slightly

*Left: THE WAY WEST: Robert Mitchum*
*Below: ONE EYED JACKS: Marlon Brando, Larry Duran*

by a typical Brando emphasis on torture and violence. Quirky incidents like Brando, interrupted by *rurales*, providently retrieving the ring, which, representing it as a priceless heirloom left him by his mother, he has just, as the last step in a seduction, slipped onto a girl's finger, or his love scene with Dad's step-daughter (Pina Pellicer) on a beach washed in copper light show an eye for visual poetry and a sure directorial hand, though the cost at which such effects were achieved blighted Brando's career as a film-maker.

Most directors respected the natural limitations of tradition and land-scape, using expanded budgets to extend Westerns only in length. Whereas the characteristic story of Fifties films had begun near its climax, Sixties Westerns were more leisurely, reaching full speed after five reels of attrac-tive landscape and relaxed character development. Richard Brooks's moody *The Professionals* (1966), a triumph for cameraman Conrad Hall, began with gunman Burt Lancaster assembling his experts, and delayed its real beginning until they had been sprung from jail or hired from their regular employers, whereupon railroad-owner Ralph Bellamy explained their task of stealing back from Mexican revolutionary Jack Palance his kidnapped wife, while *The Magnificent Seven* (John Sturges, 1960), which showed the group coming together, let audiences enter the story armed with some insight into its conflicting motivations. Based on Akira Kurosawa's *Seven Samurai*, *The Magnificent Seven* depicted a group of unemployed gunmen who accept the commission of defending a Mexican village against the annual raids by Eli Wallach's gang. In William Roberts's Hawksian script, their reasons for taking the job outline their characters. Yul Brynner is moved by the village's offer of all it has: "I've been offered a great deal before, but never everything." Steve McQueen restlessly seeks activity and employment, tyro Horst Buchholz the prestige of riding with professionals, Brad Dexter a chance at the riches that, despite Brynner's denials, he con-tinues to believe are their motive for taking so uncommercial a commission. Fugitive gunman Robert Vaughn wants asylum and an escape from his failing ability, and the cool James Coburn an opportunity to test his skill to its limit. Only Charles Bronson, half-Indian and a wanderer, sympathises with and understands the people they are to defend. Even bandit chief Wallach resembles the Seven more than he does the villagers, on whom both sides prey. "If God had not wanted them shorn," he reasons to Brynner, "he would not have made them sheep," and when at last Brynner kills him during the final battle he dies without comprehension — "But why? A man like you . . . why?" Roberts scripts in detail the tentative

*THE MAGNIFICENT SEVEN: Yul Brynner, Steve McQueen, Horst Bucholz, Charles Bronson, Robert Vaughn, Brad Dexter, James Coburn*

integration of gunmen and peasants, and the settling down of seven ego-tistical specialists into a functioning force, while Sturges gives balletic grace to the battles: peasants springing from the brush to cut down galloping bandits with billhooks; Vaughn, after waiting numb with terror, his face pressed against the stone wall, leaping into a room crowded with bandits and shooting them all in a motion as superbly choreographed as any dance routine.

In every sense a film of importance, *The Magnificent Seven* was prophetic in its commercial history. A modest $2½ million success in the US, it grossed more than $9 million world-wide, audiences responding to its violence and mythological power. Sensing a trend already started in Germany, where a number of Westerns had been made on location in Yugoslavia with expatriate American and British actors, Italian directors Sergio Leone and Duccio Tessari interested TV star Clint Eastwood in a

Western based on Kurosawa's *Yojimbo, Per un Pugno di Dollari* (*A Fistful of Dollars*, Leone, 1964). From being the graveyard of failed American *matinée* idols, the European action-picture business became a substantial source of income and prestige. The bloody school of "Spaghetti Westerns" followed, coming full circle when Ted Post made *Hang 'Em High* (1968), a Hollywood film imitating the Italian product's sadism and violence, with Clint Eastwood's bounty hunter, the victim of an unsuccessful lynching, and Pat Hingle's philosophical hanging judge exploring issues the American Western would not have encountered in its normal development. In a general stampede to cash in on the connection between Japanese costume drama and the Western, unsuspected by all but Kurosawa, whose admiration for John Ford was well known, Martin Ritt's *The Outrage* (1964) struck a flat note. On the theory that any Kurosawa film could be made into a Western, he cast Laurence Harvey, Paul Newman and Claire Bloom in a lacklustre version of *Rashomon*, which, while copying the story, missed the style and moral ambiguity of the original.

The Kurosawa imitations characterised a revision of the Western that had been going on since the mid-Fifties. For decades the doyen of the frontier film, John Ford's sentimental style and idealistic view of character had been imitated automatically by directors unable to add the quality that excused Ford's excesses, the poetic sense of landscape and symbolic precision that made even the slightest of his films a moving personal statement. Reacting against Ford, Delmer Daves and John Sturges in the Fifties reasserted the psychological style of which King Vidor had shown himself a master in *Billy the Kid* and *Duel in the Sun*, but it was left to Budd Boetticher, in a series of late-Fifties films with producer Harry Joe Brown and actor Randolph Scott (affiliated as Ranown Productions) to revive the sparse moralism of William S. Hart. The West of these films — *Seven Men From Now* (1956), *The Tall T, Decision at Sundown* (1957), *Buchanan Rides Alone* (1958), *Westbound* and *Ride Lonesome* (1959) — is the straggling fringe of the desert, the empty and miserable towns where petty tyrant, sadist and murderer hold power by default, and Boetticher's story that of a hardy survivor who seeks no trouble but, faced with an amoral adversary, disposes of him without melodrama. In at least two of the films a character says, "There are some things you can't ride around." As in Siegel, morality is reduced to a balance of force in which the most brutal crime becomes acceptable, to be forestalled only by a threat of equal retribution; reminded almost gently in *Ride Lonesome* that he hanged Scott's wife, Lee

Van Cleef murmurs with sudden memory "I almost forgot," and in *The Tall T* killer Richard Boone, discussing with his captive Scott the possibility of release, is not taken aback when Scott points out he would certainly return to kill him. "Yeah," Boone chuckles, "silly even to talk about it, ain't it?"

Although Boetticher spent much of the Sixties in enforced inactivity, his style endured in the work of young directors and writers who had worked with Ranown or on the TV series — *Wanted Dead or Alive, Gunsmoke* — that derived from his work: writers Burt Kennedy and Clair Huffaker, directors Jesse Hibbs, Andrew V. McLaglen and Vincent McEvetty who worked for Boetticher, and Sam Peckinpah whose films were made under his influence. Some quickly strayed from the rigid Ranown approach, McLaglen to big-budget Westerns — *Shenandoah* (1965), *McLintock* (1963), *The Rare Breed* (1966) — using the style, and often the actors of the John Ford films on which his father Victor had worked (and on which his son had trained as assistant director, e.g. *The Quiet Man*), without capturing anything but the superficialities of the Fordian world. Kennedy concentrated on knockabout comedy, with occasional successful essays into the traditional modes like *The Return of the Seven* (1966), a tight sequel to Sturges's classic. *The Rounders* (1965), starring Henry Fonda and Glenn Ford as seamed cowpokes, was good-natured frontier farce, and *Welcome to Hard Times* (1967) (*Killer on a Horse* in UK) returned briefly to Boetticher's plot, if not style, in the story of a town ravaged by a gunman (Aldo Ray) until Henry Fonda nervously plucks up enough courage to dispose of him. Frankly comic, *Support Your Local Sheriff* (1969) had James Garner, hero of TV's *Maverick* series, pause on his way to Australia to subdue a town with a mixture of technical ingenuity and cautious self-protection. No masterpiece, it shared *The Rounders*'s cracker-barrel humour and gave an agreeable supporting role to Joan Hackett, one of the better debutantes in *The Group*. Aside from *The Money Trap* (1966), a slick and accurate thriller about cop Glenn Ford lured by a high standard of living into a heroin theft, Kennedy's best film was *The War Wagon* (1967), based on a clever Clair Huffaker script (from his own novel) in which John Wayne and Kirk Douglas play old comrades/adversaries conspiring to steal the gold Bruce Cabot's mine owner believes to be adequately protected by an armoured coach, the "war wagon" of the title. With a tame Indian, Levi Walking Bear, delightfully played by Howard Keel, and a drunken explosives expert (Robert Walker) who tipples on whisky and nitro-glycerine, they achieve their aim in a story which, like the playing, owes much to the gangster film. Kennedy loses no opportunity to mock Western ritual — "Dumb Indians," Walking Bear grunts of his less sophisticated tribesmen — and contests of skill between Wayne and Douglas lack the conventional solemnity. After disposing of two rivals, they disagree over relative expertise. "Mine hit the ground first," Douglas points out, but Wayne has the last word. "Mine," he says, sheathing his gun, "was taller."

Sam Peckinpah seemed most likely to develop fully the sparse Boetticher Western. Many of his half-hour TV episodes (one, for *Gunsmoke*, tried out the plot of his first feature) reject the values of Sturges and Mann in favour of a bitter attitude to the West. *The Deadly Companions* (1961) resembles Boetticher in its story of a dance-hall girl (Maureen O'Hara) taking the body of her child to be buried beside that of her husband, a trek

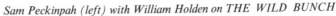

*Sam Peckinpah (left) with William Holden on THE WILD BUNCH*

on which she is accompanied by the man who accidentally killed the child (Brian Keith) and the sadistic renegades (Steve Cochran and Chill Wills) with whom Keith has a feud dating back to the Civil War, when one tried to scalp him as he lay wounded on the battlefield. Departing from the classic Westerns in that its style, while violent and naturalistic, rejects documentary realism but uses the Western landscape symbolically to emphasise an aridity of emotion, *The Deadly Companions* relates to the "new" Western, the killers stumbling through the desert carrying a child's coffin and even the essential theme of a journey to bury the dead recalling Corman or Fuller more than Ford. Peckinpah used the Boetticher style only as a springboard, much as his mentor had used the eccentric, almost surreal Westerns of Stuart Heisler (*Dallas*, *Along Came Jones*, *The Burning Hills*) and Jacques Tourneur (*Wichita*, *Stars in My Crown*).

In his second feature, Peckinpah dramatised both the extent of his imagination and the limitations it forced on him. *Ride the High Country* (1962) (*Guns in the Afternoon* in UK) used Boetticher/Heisler/Tourneur stars Randolph Scott and Joel McCrea as lawmen fighting age and the erosion of their values to protect a gold shipment. With a Fordian interest in faltering ability and moral compulsion, and echoing the soft afternoon colours Winton Hoch had created for Ford's cavalry films, it appeared to recall the great tradition, as did the stars, so accustomed to such roles that they hardly seemed to be acting. Peckinpah evoked the poignancy of declining skill and social relevance. McCrea shyly acknowledges the cheers as he rides into town, unaware that he has ambled into the path of a race whose winner the crowd is applauding. Scott, with Custer wig and automatic patter, runs a sideshow with the same bent honesty that leads him to try hijacking the gold they are hired to guard. But incidents of curious eccentricity intervene: a bar-room marriage duplicating the prayer meetings of *The Deadly Companions* and *The Ballad of Cable Hogue*; the sudden shot of a sadistic miner with a pet crow perched on his shoulder like a familiar; the dead farmer (R. G. Armstrong) who seems to pray at a grave but actually hangs on the railing, shot through the head. Appearing to respect Boetticher's stoicism, Peckinpah augments it with a fantasy that lifts his film out of the Western mainstream, suggesting a personal vision for which the form is too constricting.

While persisting with Westerns, Peckinpah further jolted his categorisation as the heir of Ford. For *The Ballad of Cable Hogue* (1970) he adopted quasi-religious fantasy, Hogue (Jason Robards) discovering a spring in the

*THE BALLAD OF CABLE HOGUE: Jason Robards Jnr.
and Stella Stevens*

desert after being abandoned by his friends, creates a prosperous way-station, then dies when Fate in the form of his prostitute/lover's automobile crushes him. David Warner as an itinerant preacher and Stella Stevens's virginal whore interrupt the Western myth, emphasising rather the contradictions in which Peckinpah delights — the desert that blooms, the virtuous prostitute — a preoccupation of which the bar-room religious service is characteristic. Baroque elements like Stevens's automobile and the funeral with silhouetted mourners and plumes contrast with a sparse desert setting, recalling Fellini rather than Ford; Peckinpah's films do, in fact, fit more comfortably in a non-American setting, hence his original decision to shoot *The Ballad of Cable Hogue* in Australia, a plan terminated when production conditions proved too primitive.

Peckinpah's surrealism and sense of the fantastic (as well as his dubious narrative skill) were less evident in *Major Dundee* (1965) and *The Wild Bunch* (1969), subjugated in the latter to a story whose conventional Western mythology and rambling dramatic structure made virtuosity difficult. Claiming to describe accurately the unpleasantness of violent

*MAJOR DUNDEE: Richard Harris*

death, he offered instead poetic evocations of violence, slow motion defusing the act of murder, a device at its best horrifically powerful, at its worst as trivial as a TV commercial for shotguns. Never given the weight Ford or Hathaway might have allocated to it, the story, of William Holden's bandit boss leading his gang on one last raid, only to be destroyed by a Mexican revolutionary army and an ex-comrade turned lawman (Robert Ryan), became lost in the welter. Of all Peckinpah's films, *Major Dundee* most impressively balances poetry and realism, unmarred even by producer Jerry Bressler, who altered Peckinpah's cutting, and refused, despite an offer by director and star to work without salary, to shoot extra scenes both men thought essential. Again using a conventional plot — a Northern officer (Heston) is forced to recruit Confederate prisoners, led by his old comrade Richard Harris, to fight a renegade Indian band — Peckinpah discards heroics to dwell on the conflict between Heston's ruthless pragmatist and the visionary flair of Harris, an Irish mercenary whose pursuit of lost causes will, he knows, end in violent death. "Damn you, Major Dundee," Harris rages. "I damn your name, I damn your flag." Ignoring the elements Ford and Wise took from this situation in *Fort Apache* and *Two Flags West*, Peckinpah concentrates on the men and their philosophical conflict. The battle is one of titans, shown in almost Biblical splendour. Seen first in a barred pit, defiant in grey uniform and plumed hat even as chains weigh him down, Harris rises to be Heston's equal and confidant until a basic incompatibility leads them to the sacrifice of an assault against impossible odds. In a lake-side love scene between Heston and Senta Berger which ends when an arrow pierces his leg, a fiesta in the square of a village where executed leaders had hung, and in a characteristic scene of dissension between the two factions in an abandoned church, Peckinpah plays on the anomalies of collaboration to evoke a shifting society where only fear, distrust and the will to death have any relevance.

Peckinpah's films and the Spaghetti cycle shared the conviction, embraced equally by Boetticher and Sturges though with contrasting results, that Western myths had lost their potency. The gunman, once revealed as a cowardly thug or weary professional, could not again attain the purity of Hopalong Cassidy. But only a few directors saw this destruction of an American myth not as a quirk of fashion but a signpost to the growing irrelevance of the frontier mythology in a culture where the brutal expediency of the gangster film more accurately reflected popular feeling. Siegel and his associates celebrated a society resembling the true West, whereas the Western had for decades lingered in a manufactured world. A few films, most of them excellent, extrapolated the purist values of the mythical West into modern settings as a means of emphasising their decline. They show the few remaining shreds of Western culture eroded and distorted by the mechanisation which, while destroying the legend of the cowboy, offered nobody in his place but the filling station attendant and the short-order cook. In David Miller's gloomy and violent *Lonely Are the Brave* (1962) Kirk Douglas's ranch hand flees with his horse into the mountains when an unfeeling law shows itself unable to understand his implied appeal for room to move, to be the poetic figure modern society has made a relic. Hunted by helicopters and squad cars, he finally dies under the wheels of a heavy truck, crushed by the forces he has tried to oppose. Like Boetticher's films and most of these "modern" Westerns, it takes as its setting the desert fringe, where, in run-down settlements, a few individualists seek desperately to retain some shreds of honour, a background employed skilfully by John Huston in *The Misfits* (1961), his sole film of the Sixties to

*THE MISFITS: Thelma Ritter, Eli Wallach*

show the imagination of earlier years. Arthur Miller's original screenplay used his wife Marilyn Monroe to express a naturalness and vitality her admirers, desert drop-outs and small-time adventurers, recognise as the spirit of a West none has ever seen, but with which they are totally entranced. Crushed, they persist in those aspects of their life that seem to them most purely honourable and manly. Eli Wallach's Guido relives his war years in a battered plane, Phonse (Montgomery Clift, giving a performance of eerie accuracy) his days as a rodeo star in contests where his punch-drunk brain and impaired reflexes make him a pitiable figure; Isabelle (Thelma Ritter) and Gay (Clark Gable) disguise the aimlessness a lack of family and ambition bring, but underneath is a despair that the open, free Roslyn (Marilyn Monroe), in Reno for her divorce, brings out. When they visit a high 'desert plateau to trap wild horses for dog-food, it is she who shows them how far from the ideal of Western life they have strayed, and in releasing the horses Gay gives not only the animals but he and the girl a further brief hold on their dream. Driving through the night, they fix their eyes on the star that leads home, a poignant scene given added sadness by being for both their last.

Paul Newman in *Hud* (Martin Ritt, 1963) and *Cool Hand Luke* (Stuart Rosenberg, 1967) characterised the modern Western hero as disoriented and anachronistic, persisting, despite the decay of ranch life in the first, and in the second a chain-gang's tortures, with a futile rebellion. *Hud*, one of the Sixties most important films and a top box-office success, explores movingly, in a terse Irving Ravetch/Harriet Frank Jnr. script, the dissolution of the Texas cattle empires and the collapse of cowboy traditions in the face of changing industrial and social conditions. Melvyn Douglas came out of retirement to create a memorable portrait of quiet indomitability as the old rancher, but it is Newman's Hud, drunken wenching heir to the range, his nephew Brandon de Wilde, initially admiring but later disillusioned by his hero's corruption and cruelty, and the arrogant sexuality of Patricia Neal as the housekeeper he lusts after but cannot possess who control the film, supported by James Wong Howe's relentlessly realistic exterior photography that bleeds the sky of character, exposing the film's characters like microbes on the sterile slide of the bleached plain.

In *Tell Them Willie Boy Is Here* (1969) Abraham Polonsky made a second Hollywood *début* after years on the anti-Red blacklist, offering another

*COOL HAND LUKE: Paul Newman*

119

parable of individuality, renegade Indian Willie Boy (Robert Blake) giving his life in protest against the inhuman confinement of his people by an unfeeling 1909 administration and its contempt for Indian customs. With his kidnapped bride (Katharine Ross) he sets off into the mountains, pursued reluctantly by sheriff Christopher Cooper (Robert Redford) whose sympathy for Willie does not prevent him from killing him at the climax; Willie, Polonsky implies, is killed not by Cooper but by the progress Cooper represents. As the sheriff becomes more agreeable to the audience and Willie more desperate, Polonsky's script turns us reluctantly from conventional sympathy for the underdog to an acceptance that a West where Presidents come on tour and townspeople are far enough from the memory of Indian uprising to view one with relish and excitement has no room for a lone Indian who believes, like his people, that a man killed in fair fight is not murdered.

The decay of Western forms did not always produce serious and original films of this calibre. Among the curious eccentricities was the highly successful *Cat Ballou* (Elliot Silverstein, 1965), Jane Fonda playing a frontier heroine and Lee Marvin a bizarre double role as drunken old-time gunman Kid Sheleen and his brother with a false silver nose, Tim Strawn. A feature *début* by TV graduate Silverstein, the film made clever use both of Western myth and stage devices like bar-room duo Stubby Kaye and Nat King Cole providing Brechtian comments in song on the action. Also cynically humorous, *Waterhole 3* (William Graham, 1967) exploited James Coburn's easy menace in a comedy role, showing his progress, via murder and rape (in his phrase "Assault with a friendly weapon"), to a buried treasure. Carroll O'Connor as Sheriff Honest John Coppercud of Integrity, Arizona, and Joan Blondell as the town *madame* gave commenable support. James Shigeta played a Chinese laundryman trained as a gunfighter by "The Deacon," a black-clothed gun-slinging lay preacher whom singer Mel Tormé made a compelling figure, in James Clavell's *Walk Like a Dragon* (1960), and Elvis Presley a half-civilized Indian in Don Siegel's *Flaming Star* (1960), the violent precision of which counterbalanced the unlikely plot, just as in *Two Mules For Sister Sarah* (1970) Siegel made believable Shirley MacLaine's dance-hall girl dressing as a nun after rapists steal her clothes, then fighting her way out of hostile territory with the help of laconic Clint Eastwood, by careful attention to the mechanics of their uneasy relationship. Gambling that proven talents from overseas would boost falling profits. Fox imported Serge Bourguignon (*Les Dimanches de*

*TWO MULES FOR SISTER SARAH: Shirley MacLaine,
Clint Eastwood*

*Ville d'Avray/Sundays and Cybele*) from France and Paramount Silvio Narrizano (*Georgy Girl*), but the Westerns each made left both studios with headaches and deficits. Fox's gesture, part of a Darryl F. Zanuck plan that also gave German Bernhard Wicki money to make *Morituri* (released, after disastrous previews, as *The Saboteur: Codename Morituri*, in 1965), was so unsuccessful that its most promising project, Akira Kurosawa's *The Day Custer Fell*, was shelved. Narizzano's *Blue* (1968), with Terence Stamp as the smouldering younger son of a Mexican bandit boss, confined itself to moody shots of Stamp prowling through Stanley Cortez's sullenly photographed desertscapes, "Method" style aptly complemented by direction of alarming mannerism. Bourguignon's *The Reward* (1965) failed, by contrast, through an excess of subtlety. A story of innocence and its destruction by the forces of logic, it struggled to assert itself as a personal statement in the face of artificial studio interiors and clumsy cutting. Bourguignon's evocation of the ageless desert landscape and incidents reminiscent in their brutality of Buñuel give *The Reward* a unique and disturbing air: a man's hand crushes in huge close-up some sleepy flies; the girl (Yvette Mimieux) wanders, rainwashed and pure, in the desert as her lovers express their lust in dream-like images, one recalling that he had always wanted to pull an angel from heaven and, tearing off her wings, alone possess her.

Ignoring crumbling standards and a cynical disregard of tradition, the Western's classic exponents persevered with familiar stories and faces, recognising that proved ability gave them an edge. Henry Hathaway, master of the action film and at last receiving his proper due, exercised his taste for balletic violence in *The Sons of Katie Elder* (1965), the Fordian plot of a frontier clan avenging the death of its weaker members given added force by Hathaway's delight in communal punch-ups and exterior gunfights. An oddity, *5 Card Stud* (1968) combined alien and conflicting elements: Robert Mitchum repeating his *Night of the Hunter* role of gun-toting and vengeful preacher, attempting on this occasion to redress the killing of a relative in a crooked card game; curious vertical crane shots and editing effects seldom seen in the Western; and an unlikely role for Inger Stevens as a lady barber with an all-girl staff. Gambler Dean Martin, commenting that the last item on her price list — "Miscellaneous: $25" — is expensive, is told "Yeah, but it sure sells well." His most successful film of the Sixties, *True Grit* (1969), tempted Hathaway to a similarly decorated approach, the antique style of Charles Portis's first-person novel of a girl hunting down the men who killed her father inviting the flippancy that marred George Roy Hill's profitable but empty *Butch Cassidy and the Sundance Kid* (1969), but ever the action specialist, Hathaway neutralised its whimsy with realistic autumn settings and blunt playing from John Wayne as the decayed lawman Rooster Cogburn, Kim Darby as the girl, and singer Glenn Campbell as an unlikely Texas ranger. In the role of a harassed horse trader, Strother Martin, the decade's finest character-acting discovery, confidently reached Wayne's standard of instinctive skill.

Hathaway's remaining Westerns disappointed. *Nevada Smith* (1966), using the portion of Harold Robbins's *The Carpetbaggers* not covered in Edward Dmytryk's sprawling 1964 adaptation, wasted Steve McQueen as the young gunman tracking down Karl Malden, who murdered and mutilated his Indian fosterparents, trading on sadism in some prison scenes and a final sanguinary encounter, where McQueen leaves Malden alive but perforated by a number of bullets, his survival the result of an eleventh hour discovery of compassion by McQueen that Malden is entitled to wish had come slightly earlier. With George Marshall and John Ford, Hathaway also directed parts of *How the West Was Won* (1962), adding some exciting fights and explosions to his sections, "The Rivers," "The Plains," and "The Outlaws," but the film's ruling influence was Ford, whose segment on the Civil War shows all the mastery of a career that began in 1917. To Ford, the Sixties offered not rest but reflection. His films of the decade echo the themes of earlier works, but even when thumbing through his album he displays a characteristically emotional and personal view of existence. A negro cavalry troop in the post-Civil War period gingerly integrates with the new American ideals in *Sergeant Rutledge* (1960), and though Ford's attitude to the Negro is patronising, landscape and character, particularly in the case of Woody Strode's honourable hero accused of rape, are precisely related. Recalling his 1956 success *The Searchers*, and sharing its theme, *Two Rode Together* (1961) uses the attempt by cavalry officer Richard Widmark and self-interested lawman James Stewart to rescue Indian captives as a means of analysing frontier morality and its erosion by urban capitalist values. The same thoughtfulness marks *The Man Who Shot Liberty Valance* (1962), a spartan work making few box-office concessions, and for this reason notably perceptive in its examination of law and order, a searching dissection extending eventually to the whole Fordian philosophy. James Stewart's political lawyer and John Wayne's instinctive man of the West embody the great forces in American mythology, Law and The Land, and Ford picks his way through the intricacies of their conflict

*THE MAN WHO SHOT LIBERTY VALANCE: Andy Devine, John Wayne, Jeanette Nolan, John Qualen, Vera Miles, James Stewart*

with complete authority. Far more serious than *Cheyenne Autumn*, his 1964 story of an Indian tribe driven to search for new lands by the brutality of white men, in which Ford succumbs to the sentimental contempt for other races that has always marred his work, *The Man Who Shot Liberty Valance* sums up the best of Sixties Westerns.

Though Howard Hawks's best films of the period are *Red Line 7000* (1965) and *Hatari!* (1962), both of which use a dangerous sport — carracing in the first, big-game trapping in the second — to present a stimulating analysis of relationships among men under pressure, and the bonds between these men and the challenging female companions Hawks has chosen and filmed with such care since his early fascination with Lauren Bacall, he created in *El Dorado* (1967) and *Rio Lobo* (1970) Westerns comparable to his classic work, particularly in the first, whose parallels to the seminal *Rio Bravo* stem, as scenarist Leigh Brackett confided, from Hawks taking a print of the earlier film on location so as not to err in his duplication. Dealing again with old comrades forming an alliance with a young

*Howard Hawks directs Robert Mitchum in EL DORADO*

man and a girl to defeat evil, *El Dorado* has the pervading sense of darkness shot with red flashes, the clashing sexual relationships and the violent humour one expects from Hawks, and which Robert Mitchum and John Wayne as the ageing central characters skilfully provide. A dimension of realism was excised from the film when the company declined to follow the original story, in which Wayne was afflicted by a heart condition that finally kills him; in the released film, his illness stems from an unlikely bullet lodged near his spine. Wayne, unpleasantly corpulent for his role as a Civil War Northern major hunting the bandits who killed some of his men during the robbery of a gold train, ambled comfortably through *Rio Lobo*, leading some critics to comment that the parade of athletically ravishing young women — Elsa Martinelli, Laura Devon, Michèle Carey, Jennifer O'Neill — in Hawks's Sixties films, the continuing character of John Wayne and the delight in cinematic toys like the elaborate inventions of Red Buttons in *Hatari!* and the train crash of *Rio Lobo* marked an artistic senility. But to those who know this director's work the sense is rather that of a great artist avoiding the doubt and recrimination into which John Ford strayed, and relishing instead the pleasures of a form and skill in which he has few masters.

# 9. Menopause Love

HOLLYWOOD PRODUCTION programmers, who had long recognised not one but a number of audiences, viewed with alarm the increasing fragmentation of the film-going public. Increased spending power among the under-seventeens and a new demand from the normally anti-cinema intellectual minority for films tailored to its needs created two new markets Hollywood never succeeded in satisfying; its sole success was to accommodate the newly rich and leisured rural audience with bucolic comedies — *Did You Hear the One about the Travelling Saleslady?*, *The Ghost and Mr. Chicken*, *The Shakiest Gun in the West* — featuring the grotesque Phyllis Diller and Don Knotts. Daunted by the demands of the 18–25 age group, by far the most potentially lucrative, studios catered to the less sophisticated 12–17 audience with the elements — pop music, mild sex, broad comedy, surfing and cars — that had proven attraction, though here the lack of trained young stars hampered their efforts. Producers competed for the few TV graduates and pop singers showing a shred of ability, and Fox even revived for a few months the obsolete "talent school" idea, dazzled by the success Universal had achieved with its one-woman sub-teen department, Sandra Dee, who giggled her way through the profitable *Gidget* (1959) — followed by Deborah Walley in *Gidget Goes Hawaiian* (1961) and Cindy Carol in *Gidget Goes to Rome* (1963), directed in each case by a ludicrously misused Paul Wendkos — and who also inherited Debbie Reynolds's cast-off role for *Tammy Tell Me True* and *Tammy and the Doctor* (Harry Keller, 1961 and 1963), romances so saccharine that Peter Fonda, co-star of the second, claimed he was physically ill after its *première*.

The shrewd American-International team of Samuel Z. Arkoff and James Nicholson that had, albeit doubtfully, financed Roger Corman in his eccentric career, mounted an ambitious campaign to conquer the teen market, exploiting three *genres* — horror/science fiction, pop musical and surfing comedy — which became in time hopelessly muddled. *Beach Party* (William Asher, 1963) used Mickey Mouse Club cast-off Annette Funicello and some inexpensive pop groups in a sex comedy set mainly on a Californian beach, a formula so successful it was repeated four times a year until the mid-Sixties. Buster Keaton, coaxed out of semi-retirement, clowned pathetically in *Pajama Party* (Don Weis, 1964), *Muscle Beach*

*Party* (William Asher, 1964), *Beach Blanket Bingo* and *How to Stuff a Wild Bikini* (both Asher, 1965). Crossed with Corman horror, the form produced *The Ghost in the Invisible Bikini*, and Corman regular Vincent Price starred in probably the only valuable film of the cycle, *Doctor Goldfoot and the Bikini Machine* (Norman Taurog, 1965), a vast in-joke for the horror buffs with Price as the megalomaniac Doctor G. wiring a number of nubile A-I starlets as robot bombs designed to blow up unwitting lovers; Price described the cast as "myself and every high-breasted woman in Hollywood." His castle is decorated with "ancestral portraits" of Price in some earlier roles, including Fuller's *The Baron of Arizona*, while the climax re-uses set-designer Daniel Haller's clanking torture machine from *The Pit and The Pendulum*.

With even mildly amusing conceits like *Doctor Goldfoot* greeted with blank disinterest by the teenage audience, it is not surprising that films of serious intent disappeared without trace. Among scores of impoverished pop musicals, Bob Rafelson's *Head* (1968), written and produced by *Easy Rider*'s Jack Nicholson, received little comment. Bypassing the meagre talents of its stars, The Monkees, an artificial group manufactured as an American equivalent of The Beatles, its surrealism baffled actors and audience alike. Intercutting images of an executed Vietnamese prisoner with advertisements and fantasy sequences, some making imaginative use of multi-image and solarisation, accompanying songs with dazzling colour and slow-motion, pushing the baffled group into fake fights at a film studio on which the *Head* crew appear to become involved, then jumping, via a bizarre scene of a cop making himself up as a woman, to the ultimate parody of *Help!* where, to top Paul McCartney as a miniature among the cigarette butts, all four Monkees become dandruff on somebody's shoulder, Rafelson and Nicholson show the imagination that was to produce their highly successful *Five Easy Pieces* (1971). Many of Walt Disney's live-action features used sub-teen plots with charm and skill. *Pollyanna* (David Swift, 1960), *The Moonspinners* (James Neilson, 1964) and *The Parent Trap* (David Swift, 1961) exploited Hayley Mills's slight talent, though only the first, with its picture of a sunny rural landscape in more peaceful times, completely succeeded. *Where the Boys Are* (Henry Levin, 1960), a parody of Glendon Swarthout's lively novel, had clever playing from Paula Prentiss and Jim Hutton as college students breaking out in Fort Lauderdale, and captured the frantic mood of an American resort bulging with noisy, unwinding teenagers. Horror film specialist Jack Arnold directed

127

*HIGH SCHOOL CONFIDENTIAL: Russ Tamblyn, Diane Jergens*

*High School Confidential* (1960) with style and tension, hampered by the unlikely story of an undercover FBI man (Russ Tamblyn) investigating drug trafficking in a high school, a racket engineered by former child star Jackie Coogan. Tamblyn cruising on campus, shaving from an electric razor plugged into the console of his convertible, or a bed covered with three weeping blondes (Jan Sterling, Mamie Van Doren, Diane Jergens) after all have been beaten by the gang in its quest for information, show Arnold's assured touch and instinctive erotic precision.

*WILD SEED: Michael Parks*

All these films tempted the teenage audience with variations on a familiar pattern, and only Universal gambled on the hope that young directors working in the idiom popularised by the French *nouvelle vague* might catch, as in Europe, the imagination of the entire under-30 audience. UCLA Film School graduate Brian G. Hutton and young Canadian TV director Harvey Hart were each offered the opportunity to make a feature with relative freedom from studio control. Hutton's *Wild Seed* (1965) (*Fargo* in UK),

129

with new star Michael Parks as a wandering drop-out and Celia Kaye as the runaway girl he befriends, used documentary style and Mid-Western locations with obvious flair. Sequences of life on the road — the brutality of police who round up and terrorise the tramps, an excitingly shot and scored sequence of hopping a speeding freight train — have remarkable veracity, as does Hutton's picture of New York at dawn, steam dribbling from street gratings as the girl sets off in search of her father. Hart's *Bus Riley's Back in Town* (1965), based on one of William Inge's less effective screenplays, is highly coloured and romantic, using Universal's familiar country town backlot sets, but its sincerity, technical skill and courageous attempt on some of the themes explored by Penn in *The Chase* suggested a promising talent. Parks again starred, this time as a dissident hell-raiser who returns from Navy service anxious to improve his life. Scorning his old garage mechanic job, he considers one as assistant to a mortician, who alarms him at their interview by pressing his hand companionably but constantly on his knee, briefly helps Brad Dexter's home fumigation expert before becoming a salesman in his own right, particularly successful with lonely housewives, but succumbs at last to his old girlfriend Ann-Margret, now grass widow of the local millionaire, becoming, as before, a servant and stud, roles for which he has an instinctive affinity. After rejecting Ann-Margret, he finds the prospect of a job in the garage and marriage to home-town girl Janet Margolin attractive, and sinks at the conclusion into comfortable anonymity. The Universal project ended abruptly when box-office returns from *Fargo* manifested the film as a disaster, and Universal determined to hedge its bet on *Bus Riley* by adding new scenes for Ann-Margret (shot by an anonymous director, they stand out glaringly). So many cuts and changes were demanded that Inge removed his name from the credits, and Hart turned to a successful TV career in the US and Canada and late-Sixties return to features, his reaction to the debacle, "It was an experience," perhaps echoing Universal's

As the teenage market basked in the competition for its money, the important 18–25 group remained largely indifferent to cinema until *The Graduate*'s success in 1968 dramatised the fact to Hollywood that its sights had always been set too low. Only Frank Perry with *David and Lisa* (1963) anticipated the obsession with tortured youth, sexual maturity and the plight of the adolescent intellectual that sustained Nichols's film, and Perry, like Nichols, was a New Yorker, working outside the Hollywood system. For most of the Sixties, Hollywood's only appeal to this lucrative audience had been outspoken romances in which an attractive young couple fight the scepticism of their parents to find true love. Douglas Sirk's formidable talent had exploited the lurking eroticism of such stories in the Fifties, but no Sixties director competed with these baroque gems. Jean Negulesco's *Jessica* (1962) used the delightful Angie Dickinson as a young American midwife fighting the prejudice of a Sicilian village to catch her man, the local Count, but its appeal was mainly to older filmgoers who remembered Negulesco's Forties melodramas. Delmer Daves adapted more effectively in *A Summer Place* (1960) and *Parrish* (1961), vehicles for eternal freshman Troy Donohue but enlivened by Daves's deft touch, Max Steiner scores of lyric efficiency and carefully chosen rural locations. In *A Summer Place*, Donohue, son of Arthur Kennedy's educated, alcoholic New England hotelier, has an affair with tourist Sandra Dee until her mother, a reptilian Constance Ford, comes close to breaking it up, while in *Parrish* his impoverished mother (Claudette Colbert) takes a job as companion to the spoiled daughter of Karl Malden's tobacco magnate. Appalled by Malden's snobbish family, Parrish retreats among the tobacco men, taking over the failing farm of idealist Dean Jagger, and marrying Malden's emancipated younger daughter. Daves's locations — a rocky Cape Cod promontory for the first, sultry East Coast valleys for the second — balance and neutralise the simple sentiment of his stories.

Among producers searching for the commercial lodestone in a confused market, Universal's Ross Hunter, after fabulous success with the sex comedy and *Tammy* series, thought to exploit the opposite end of the age range with remakes of successful melodramas aimed at the over-fifties. Hunter agreed that his policy of using Forties *matinée* queens in films that refused to acknowledge their decrepitude would be quickly terminated by the years: "My next picture is going to be called *Menopause Love*," he told critic Charles Higham in 1966, "and the one after that *The Wheel Chair*, and the one after that *The Stretcher.* . . ." None of the admirable troupers Hunter chose for his productions showed, in fact, any of the expected infirmity. Lana Turner excelled in *Portrait in Black* (Michael Gordon, 1960), playing Anthony Quinn's lover and co-murderer of her crippled husband, and dominated *Madame X* (David Lowell Rich, 1966), most opulent of the cycle, as a woman who flees from a manslaughter charge, abandons her child, but returns to save his life in a tearful courtroom climax. Like *Back Street* (David Miller, 1961) a second remake, the success of *Madame X* encouraged Hunter to plan a third *Dark Angel*, in which

Merle Oberon had enchanted 1935 audiences, but a decline in box-office returns made this inadvisable. Less sensitive to his stars' vanity, Robert Aldrich, doyen of the brutal thriller, saw potential in venerable ladies whose box-office potential outran their looks, casting two of them, Bette Davis and Joan Crawford, in *Whatever Happened to Baby Jane?* (1962), a sado-gerontophilic exercise in Hollywood *Grand Guignol* about forgotten child star Baby Jane (Davis), a wrinkled crone, lurking in her Thirties mansion, attended by crippled sister (Crawford) and obese pianist (Victor Buono) who recreate for her the ancient world. Aldrich, adopting a style perfected by Robert Siodmak and cameraman Nicholas Musuraca for Forties thrillers like *The Spiral Staircase*, mirrors the sham, the fanatical defence of illusions and the hard-edged, repellent Californian environment on which Hollywood subsists, dusty ringing tile floors, wrought iron screens choked with vegetation and stifling shadows evoking the corruption of a decayed culture. *Hush . . . Hush, Sweet Charlotte* (1965) moved the location to a rotting Southern mansion, with Bette Davis the *belle* whose experiences on the night of her *début*, involving the murder of a lover with a meat cleaver, freeze her permanently in the past. Olivia de Havilland and her lover Joseph Cotten plan a nightmare assault on Charlotte, culminating in Cotten's appearance on the staircase dripping and wreathed in water weed after an apparent drowning, yet another homage by Hollywood to Clouzot's seminal *Les Diaboliques*. Other directors explored this narrow form, Olivia de Havilland appearing in Walter Grauman's *Lady in a Cage* (1964) as a dowager trapped in her private lift by juvenile delinquents, and Joan Crawford wasted her time in roles as mask-faced scientist or matron. Aldrich remained the master of his created *genre*, refusing to admit its exhaustion, varying it only slightly in *The Legend of Lylah Clare* (1968) which explored the polluted Hollywood environment in a story recalling Josef von Sternberg's elevation of Marlene Dietrich to stardom. Finch as the bearded, obsessive director and Kim Novak as his languid discovery conveyed much of that odd relationship while corresponding only occasionally with the facts; the resemblance, as in the grotesque knife murder at the climax and Lylah's fall down the curving marble staircase of her Hollywood mansion, is less to real life than to Sternberg's unique films.

Aldrich's films, as well as *Parrish* and *A Summer Place*, emphasised the widening gap between effective and commercially viable stars of late middle-age and young newcomers whose main appeal was in their physical attractiveness, but the popularity even of abysmal romances starring the most provocative of these young stars brought home to Hollywood a further ruling influence in the production of big-budget melodrama, the growing interest among audiences in the sexual activities of the new generation. A lessening of censorship in the Fifties allowed studios for the first time to exploit such subjects, and the Sixties audience, predominantly middle-aged, was eager for films illustrating its preoccupation. Sex comedies satisfied them to some extent with films in which mature men wallowed in luxury and sensuality, but few producers took the cue that a market for May/September sex subjects was waiting to be tapped, a profitable field at last conceded by default to the French and Italians. George Cukor's *The Chapman Report* (1962), based on Irving Wallace's gloss of Kinsey, gingerly exposed rampant suburban sexuality, with bored housewives relieving their frustrations with beach bums and tradesmen, but although Cukor's proven ability in directing female stars extracted fine performances from Claire Bloom and Shelley Winters, prudery and censorship damaged the film as they had *Kiss Me, Stupid*.

*Jeff Corey and Olivia De Havilland in LADY IN A CAGE*

Unable or unwilling to see that sex comedy's outspoken themes could, with a little juggling, be adapted to melodrama, Hollywood produced not the expected flood of exploitation pictures but a few serious and sincere dramas in which the problems of urban sex were examined with real insight, tributes to the perception of young directors who seized the opportunity of a tentatively permissive climate and a production vacuum. *Private Property* (Leslie Stevens, 1960) explored the boredom and tensions of a middle-class housewife made the prey of two layabouts, capably played by Corey Allen and Warren Oates, and Alexander Singer, embracing a theme he was to use constantly through the Sixties, made *A Cold Wind in August* (1961), a brutal, compassionate picture of the affair between an ageing stripper and young slum kid. Singer analyses both the misplaced maternal instinct and obsession with age that drives the woman (Lola Albright) to take up with the boy (Scott Marlowe), and the conflicting desires that attract him. Few Americans have shown Singer's sure grasp of sexual attitudes. Albright, the erotic dream of all men, views her night-time duties with professional detachment, provoking her audience with cold efficiency, the mask of her face and her calculated movements extinguishing all emotion. Preparing herself privately for her young lover, she is equally skilful, perfuming her body, slipping into loose clothes, murmuring compliments on her beauty in a narcissistic devotional. The classic *hetaira*, she repels the boy with the frankness of her skill as a stripper, and he accepts the invitation of a teenage tart for a bout of heavy necking instead. Although he explored the same ideas in *Psyche '59* (1964, in England) and *Love Has Many Faces* (1965), a hilariously overheated frolic among Acapulco beach society with hirsute Hugh O'Brien cutting a swathe through the sagging socialites, *A Cold Wind in August* remains his most interesting film.

Also exploiting, though only in passing, the aphrodisiac value of an age differential, Curtis Harrington's *Games* (1967) employed Simone Signoret, archetypal "older woman" in a number of English-language films aiming to cash in on her undeniable appeal even in middle-age, as the star of a thriller which, like *Les Diaboliques* (in which she had also starred), crossed crime with sexual obsession. New York dilettantes James Caan and Katherine Ross adopt refugee Signoret, making her a permanent guest in their pop-art crammed town house. From jokes played on the husband by the two bored women, and by the couple in retaliation on their guest, a cycle of games grows up, bizarre charades where, in grinning "Benda Masks" (designed by Emile Benda in the Twenties for Florenz Ziegfield

134

*GAMES: Simone Signoret*

and worn by showgirls in his tableaux) they act out ritual executions as neon sculptures flicker and antique pin-ball machines flash. A remarkable atmosphere in the first half, of guilt, boredom and perversion, excuses the *Grand Guignol* of the climax; one remembers best Caan's alarm as he discovers what appears to be a sordid afternoon affair between his wife and a delivery boy (Don Stroud), actually a joke engineered by Signoret, and his revenge, an apparently violent tiff whose elements, as the couple gleefully demonstrate, are an improvised argument and the thwack of a belt against the door-jamb. In each case the wife is a pawn, telegraphing the affinity between Signoret and Caan that leads them to plot her destruction, a scheme in which only the house, inhabited by grim sculptures within and whirling dead leaves without, remains coldly neutral, the real villain of this curious film.

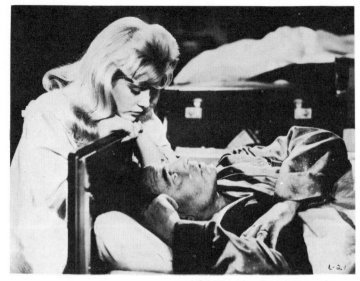

*LOLITA: Sue Lyon, James Mason*

Affairs between older women and young men, actually less common in real life than the reverse, often penetrated the censorship smoke screen, encouraged by the success of French films like Autant-Lara's *Le Blé en Herbe,* but Hollywood seldom allowed older men to be seen exercising their attraction over nubile young girls. Preminger's *The Moon Is Blue*, using a coy version of such a relationship, had to defy the lack of an MPPA certificate and widespread community resistance to achieve release, and the most potent expression in prose of such a relationship, Vladimir Nabokov's *Lolita*, defeated big-budget production until M-G-M backed Stanley Kubrick's British filming of an emasculated script. Superbly professional, with a remarkable recreation in England of the book's obsession with freeways, drive-ins and the depersonalised American society, Kubrick's *Lolita* (1962) suffered from cautious casting. However effective we find James Mason and Peter Sellers, Sue Lyon is decidedly too mature for Nabokov's pre-pubescent nymphet. Only Tuesday Weld, that rarest of Sixties phenomena, a talented young actress, had the necessary blend of innocence and carnality for this role. Wasted after her graduation from model work on some fatuous sub-teen exploitation films, she showed her talent briefly in José Ferrer's balanced and calmly professional *Return to Peyton Place* (1961) before scoring in some popular but thoughtful roles. In *Bachelor Flat* (Frank Tashlin, 1962), she was an obstinate college girl lurking in the beach-front apartment of Professor Terry-Thomas to further her romance with handsome hanger-on Richard Beymer. Impatient of explanations, she switches from casual teenager twisting her way through the chores to a fake delinquent describing with relish her fictitious exploits, a performance of remarkable flexibility and charm which she equalled in George Axelrod's *Lord Love a Duck* (1966), a comedy whose incisive satire on the American malaise, puzzling to audiences and distributors alike, led to undeservedly poor release. As the high school *belle* courted by slightly unhinged Roddy McDowall, her starry-eyed desire for a dozen cashmere sweaters, a beach holiday, a handsome husband, a movie contract — in short, all the insubstantial ideals of a cotton candy culture — expresses precisely the brainlessness of teenage society, but underlies it with an incautious ebullience and eroticism that makes the character briefly real. For Ralph Nelson in *Soldier in the Rain* (1963) she was another high-school girl entering a touching relationship with Jackie Gleason's melancholy soldier, attracted (in a classic wish-fulfilment exercise of all fat men) by the hero struggling to get out, the "Randolph Scott," as she put it, inside. Steve McQueen's role of the dedicated poker player in *The Cincinatti Kid* (1965), Norman Jewison's sub-*Hustler* exploration of big-time gambling, in this case high-stake cards in the pre-war South, overshadowed her small part as his unsophisticated girlfriend, though their visit to an overgrown farm and her attempts to interest her pre-occupied lover in her discovery of subtitled foreign movies show acting skill, as well as the simplicity and sexual attraction that were to work against her in the late Sixties, when Noel Black's *Pretty Poison* (1968) and John Frankenheimer's *I Walk the Line* (1970) wastefully miscast her as an amoral nymphet, the sort of role to which, in *Lolita*, she might have brought her undoubted talent.

No film more concisely sums up Hollywood's continuing failure to gauge the emerging young adult audience than *Easy Rider* (1969), Dennis Hopper's lyrical and exciting hymn to his generation. Claiming to reject Hollywood traditions, *Easy Rider* is in fact the most stylishly professional of all Hollywood films, with director, writer and star all trained in the

*EASY RIDER: Dennis Hopper and Peter Fonda*

studio system, and a plot clear-headedly constructed to gain popular success. "It isn't hard to make a successful movie," Hopper has said. "You just feed the elements into your computer and the answers come out." Even while making his appeal for a freer life, a less paranoid American society and a return to the sensuous freedom enjoyed in the America of an earlier age, Hopper and writer Jack Nicholson evoke the fashionable music of the day, the glamour of the motor cycle, the trendy social phenomena — communes, pot-smoking, acid — whose virtues appear, superficially, to typify the best of the drop-out philosophy. The result is a film which, like *The Graduate*, offers escapism in the disguise of social commitment, but this is not to invalidate either the skill of *Easy Rider*'s makers or the essential seriousness of their intentions. It is a tribute to Hopper and Nicholson that they recognise the traditions of Hollywood are not so easily discarded, that a language, however ill-formed or illogical, remains an instrument no artist can afford to ignore. Under the journey of Hopper's two outlaws across America — he specifically denies their status as heroes; "they're outlaws, as the men who kill them are outlaws" — is both an evocation of the pure life that can exist in the United States and a condemnation of the elements, chiefly heroin addiction, racial and social intolerance, and capitalism which can destroy everything beautiful in that life. That a film of such force should have been made by the son of a major Hollywood star trained as a juvenile in teenage romances, by a character actor in Westerns with experience almost totally in this *genre*, and by a writer whose background in cinema consisted mainly of production credits on two Monte Hellman Westerns, a rock musical and second-billing to Boris Karloff in two Roger Corman horror films merely confirms one's faith in the essential indestructability and merit of the Hollywood tradition.

# 10. Plastic Fantastic

FOR A decade preoccupied with horror and violent death, the Sixties is curiously bare of films dealing with these subjects in a mythological or fantastic context. Hollywood's exploitation of violence and sadism lacked the poetic parallel of a horror or fantasy cycle such as Warners provided for its realist dramas of the Thirties, where *The Roaring Twenties* and *I Am a Fugitive from a Chain Gang* were balanced by *Mystery of the Wax Museum* and *Doctor X*. This process, which had tended to neutralise the impact of death by evoking its aspects of poetry and dark humour, became fragmented in the Sixties, appearing arbitrarily in some inappropriate films. At one end of the spectrum, it enlivened films like *The Wild Bunch*, which used slow motion to fantasise the moment of death, and Robert Aldrich's *The Dirty Dozen* (1967), a bloodthirsty romp for a commando group composed of a military prison's sweepings, whose climax, a Götterdämerung of explosions, showed an almost obscene relish in destruction, emulated by Brian G. Hutton in his *Where Eagles Dare* (1969). *Castle Keep* (Sydney Pollack, 1969) explicitly blended the European Campaign with fantasy elements to underline the irony of an army destroying the civilisation for which the war is allegedly fought. Americans defending a medieval French castle are enthralled by the richness of the masterpieces within its walls, lured into a dream of sexual fulfilment, peace and content from which even their destruction at the hands of the enemy cannot wake them; as in the classic horror films, death succeeds life with no change in awareness. Contrasted with these oddities, masters of the fantasy film, most notably Roger Corman, persisted with elegant period myths, avoiding the sadistic relish that marred hybrids; Corman's sponsorship by American-International, a company which in its low budget/high entertainment response to public taste reflected Warner's in the Thirties, permitted him to raise the horror film to new heights of precision and subtlety.

Inflation of B-movie themes to A-budget status gave science fiction effects technicians for the first time resources equal to their task of creating the alien and the futuristic. Nothing in the Fifties equals the lavish sets of *Fantastic Voyage* (Richard Fleischer, 1966), in which explorers shrunk to microscopic size battle through the human body to repair a brain lesion. Special effects eclipse a meagre plot: lungs like ballroom-sized bellows, the

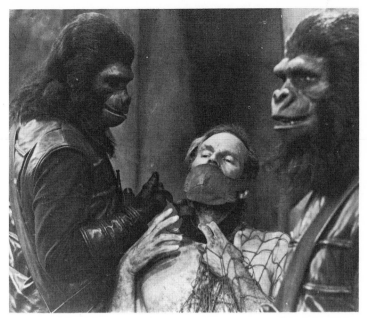

*Charlton Heston and gorilla guards in PLANET OF THE APES*

heart an echoing white cavern with a pulsing valve as its gate, veils flashing with electricity to represent the interior of the brain. *Planet of the Apes* (Franklin J. Schaffner, 1968), highly successful for Fox, relied initially on Pierre Boulle's social satire of a planet where monkeys rule and men are the oppressed savages, but two sequels — *Beneath the Planet of the Apes* (Ted Post, 1970) and *Escape from the Planet of the Apes* (Don Taylor, 1971) — rushed into production soon after, deteriorated as monkey make-up and the anachronism of talking chimpanzees imitating human attitudes coarsened the message. George Pal's *The Time Machine* (1960) set an Oscar-winning standard of effects with ingenious use of stop motion and a period time machine of red plush and brass, and the skill was continued by Byron Haskin in *Robinson Crusoe on Mars* (1964), space hardware and Death Valley settings evoking the terrors and excitements of a Martian castaway. Guaranteed good returns by a growing public interest in the space race, astronautical films thrived. *Marooned* (John Sturges, 1970), the story of three astronauts stranded in orbit, incorporated an extended apologia for space flight expenditure, and gained substantial publicity when the Apollo-13 failure conveniently coincided with general release, but meticulous recreations of a Cape Canaveral launch did not neutralise flat and predictable acting. More imaginative, if less generously financed, *Countdown* (Robert Altman, 1968) used talented newcomers James Caan and Robert Duvall in a story combining *Marooned*'s documentary realism with a perceptive look at the problems of sending a man alone through space to beat a Russian crew to the Moon. Frictions among members of the team are carefully drawn, restricted but appropriate use made of hardware, and the tensions between hard-driving teacher Duvall and dumb pupil Caan rigorously pursued by a director whose later *M\*A\*S\*H* (1970) was to make him a major name.

Films relating technology to contemporary problems seldom went beyond plush versions of the bomb-scare films so popular in the nervous Fifties. Still working in Europe, Stanley Kubrick created *Dr. Strangelove or How I Learned to Stop Worrying and Love the Bomb* (1964), a nightmare comedy on the global balance of terror, whose similarities to Sidney Lumet's *Fail Safe* (1964) caused the latter's producers to consider a lawsuit for plagiarism. Unconcerned, Kubrick continued with the exploration of science fiction as an expression of his personal ethic, making in *2001: A Space Odyssey* (1968, again in England) the cult film of the age. Overshadowed by competitors at the time, *Fail Safe* better resists the years, Lumet's nervous shooting inside the cramped war headquarters exercising a grim fascination. John Frankenheimer's *Seven Days in May* (1964) underlaid the recreation of a military plot to overthrow President Frederic March with a subliminal comment on the growing power, even intelligence, of our technological environment, extending the message of *Dr. Strangelove* and *Fail Safe* — that human control of technology must eventually lead to a tragic accident — to suggest that the machines, becoming aware of their power, may dictate their own decisions through their ability to put into any skilled hands the weapons of destruction.

Few films implied that one man or group of men could stem this tide. Our only answer, most suggested, was to be prepared. *Panic in Year Zero* (1962), efficiently directed by star Ray Milland, showed an urban family reacting with heartless efficiency to the problems of survival after atomic

*THE MANCHURIAN CANDIDATE: Frank Sinatra, Janet Leigh*

attack, and James H. Harris's *The Bedford Incident* (1965) a microcosm of national types facing world disaster when American and Russian vessels meet in an Arctic confrontation. Frankenheimer's superb *The Manchurian Candidate* (1962), in a script of force and sensitivity from George Axelrod, analysed the planting of a Communist killer in the highest circles of American government who has been programmed to murder a politician and guarantee the elevation of a Red Chinese stooge to the Presidency. A key film in modern cinema — its importance has been compared to that of *Citizen Kane* in the new depth it brought to Hollywood acting styles — with uniformly effective performances from Frank Sinatra, Laurence Harvey, Janet Leigh, James Gregory and Angela Lansbury, *The Manchurian Candidate* discards slick drama to explore the human impact of psychological manipulation. The blandness of Karl Malden's *Time Limit* (1957), whose plot and even the role of buddah-like Chinese inquisitor Kheigh Deigh anticipate those of Frankenheimer's film dramatises the latter's instinctive understanding of psychological war and its dangers, his

RETARDATIO

*THE POWER: George Hamilton*

belief in the necessity for mental as well as physical freedom. These themes were further explored in *Seconds* (1966), showing an executive (John Randolph), hungry for new sensations and a return to youth, taking a complete rejuvenation that leaves him (now played by Rock Hudson) with his old attitudes and needs unchanged. Logic demands, but mind and soul obstinately refuse to submit. Hardly in the same class, but deft and exciting, Byron Haskin's *The Power* (1968), in which a supermind invades an institute studying human responses and sets out to destroy those members of the staff who suspect its presence, broke new ground in the integration of social problems with science fiction, but unimaginative producers were reluctant to exploit the breakthrough.

As science fiction films enjoyed a brief revival, horror and fantasy suffered in a market obsessed with quick profit. The best films stemmed from the work of an individual in whose unique style others chose to work. Joseph Stefano, screenwriter and producer, became famous with his transformation of a competent Robert Bloch chiller into Alfred Hitch-

*PSYCHO: Anthony Perkins*

cock's *Psycho* (1960), first of the Sixties' clinical horrors. *Psycho*, discarding Gothic trimmings which time has robbed of all but a vestigial power, used elements from the modern world that evoked the same instinctive chill Nineteenth century readers had felt at the mention of ghosts, demons and physical torture, then still sufficiently part of the common heritage to evoke horror. Hichcock dwelt on modern obscenities of whose reality the newspapers make us daily more aware — the car crash, the axe murder, the sex killing. Although horror film techniques sustain Hitchcock's style, the ambiance, reinforced by Bernard Herrmann's whimpering, shrieking score (rare in that it is written entirely for strings; the emphasis on high and low registers suggests, in his words, "black and white music" for a black and white film), is of palpable fear, the shock of death in familiar surroundings. (A similar attitude dominated *The Birds*, 1963, Evan Hunter's script about a revolt by the birds showing, as in *Psycho*, the familiar turning on man, and savaging him for his complacency.) After *Psycho*'s success Stefano took over the excellent TV series *The Outer*

*Limits*, creating a style of subtle horror unknown since Val Lewton, and although little of this seeped into the cautious Hollywood cinema, his script for *Eye of the Cat* (David Lowell Rich, 1969), in which a fear of cats is used to destroy Eleanor Parker's San Francisco dowager, combined imagination with bloody horror.

Following *The Innocents* (1961), Jack Clayton's version of Henry James's "The Turn of the Screw," producers showed more sympathy for ghost stories of this elegant simplicity. TV series like *The Outer Limits* and *Thriller* in which John Brahm, Gerd Oswald and other Germanic stylists had been employing this style for years considered new programmes or features made from their best work, but few succeeded commercially. Spin-off pilots, in which individual episodes were boosted to ninety minutes for theatrical release, are among the Sixties' most elusive treasures. Of those that did achieve even limited distribution, *Dark Intruder* (Harvey Hart, 1965) in which a Sumerian demon terrorises San Francisco, was among the more convincing, and Ray Russell's pilot script for a series based on the Michael Curtiz classic *Mystery of the Wax Museum* emerged as the stylish *Chamber of Horrors* (Hy Averback, 1966), with Patrick O'Neal playing a mass murderer in Victorian London, his artificial hand conveniently interchangeable with instruments of death. In England, M-G-M backed Michael Anderson (later replaced by J. Lee Thompson) in *Eye of the Devil* (1966) with Deborah Kerr (replacement for Kim Novak, injured in a horse fall on location) as the wife of French count David Niven whose respect for the ancient customs of his family leads to his ritual death, a sacrifice for the fertility of the land. A smooth exercise in tension, with robed figures drifting through an antique *château* to Gary McFarland's imaginative jazz score for solo harp, it becomes minor by comparison with Robert Wise's *The Haunting* (1963), also made on English locations. In the framework of an investigation by scientist Richard Johnson and his team of mediums into the ghosts of a doomed old house, Wise plays, as he did in his Forties classics *Curse of the Cat People* and *The Body Snatcher*, on the basic fears of desertion, darkness and the unknown. A door pulses frantically like a huge heart, mysterious messages are scrawled on the walls, a ghostly hand grasps that of a lost girl as she lies in the dark of a haunted bedroom. Julie Harris and Claire Bloom as fearful medium and lesbian protector overshadow the rest of the cast but Wise's intricate cutting to show an inter-relation between the house's sinister architecture and its victims' growing fear achieves remarkable effects.

*EYE OF THE DEVIL: Deborah Kerr*

Roman Polanski's *Rosemary's Baby* (1968) offers competition to *The Haunting* as the Sixties' best story of the supernatural, and though the setting, an old New York apartment house, and story, of the anti-Christ born to a young housewife, appear opposites to those of Wise's film, both films take their force from the emotions of their trapped and vulnerable heroines. William Fraker's photography and Polanski's precise direction

147

of Mia Farrow as the wife and John Cassavetes as her evilly manipulated husband, but perhaps most persuasively Ruth Gordon and Sidney Blackmer as the apparently charming next-door neighbours who reveal themselves as agents of the devil, create a rich sense of implicit evil contained in the simplest surroundings, the core of Ira Levin's impressive original novel. Even a love scene between Rosemary and her husband achieves a sinister air — the city looms coldly outside the window, the bare boards seem mocking and false, a stage set soon to be struck, revealing leering observers behind.

Fantasy, as opposed to horror, had few Sixties exponents. Jack Smight's *The Illustrated Man* (1969) attempted a visual expression of three atmospheric Ray Bradbury stories, but only the framing situation, of an elaborately tattooed tramp (Rod Steiger) recalling his encounter with a rural witch (Claire Bloom) and her "illustration" of his body, conveys Bradbury's melancholy style. Of the stories, "The Day It Rained Forever"

*Jack Smight with Rod Steiger in THE ILLUSTRATED MAN*

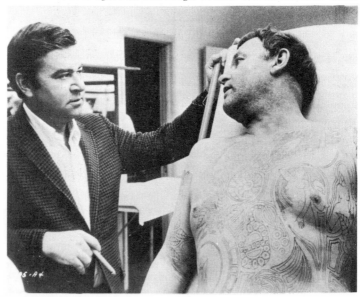

depends on the realistic evocation of a planet on which rain falls so heavily that a man might drown if he turned his face upwards, a feat the effects department had little hope of achieving, while the third, "The Last Night of the World," vaguely defined by billowing pavilions and tranquil meadows, did little to suggest two people at the twilit end of the planet's existence. However, in "The Veldt," Smight captured a little of Bradbury's horror at the amorality and sadism of children, an effect neutralised by the aseptic discomfort of his plastic future environment, as bad a guess at 1990 modes as *Just Imagine* was of 1970. Hoping to cash in on another American mystic, George Pal adapted Charles Finney's "The Circus of Doctor Lao" as *The Seven Faces of Doctor Lao* (1964), Tony Randall's peripatetic Eastern mystic changing masks and personalities to bewitch and reform a small Western town. William Tuttle's masks deservedly received a special Academy Award, and were circulated as an exhibition to launch the film.

Roger Corman, independent, uneven master of fantasy, made the Sixties' most ambitious exercises in the macabre. Not true horror films, his American-International fantasies discarded Gothic for the flamboyant Renaissance mode. Recognising in Poe the threads that link his work to medieval romance, Corman exploited colour, mood and imagery rather than the grisly plots, achieving a Baudelaireian vivacity and eroticism. *The Masque of the Red Death* (1964, in England), his most lavish production, had the grotesquerie of a Florentine entertainment: a dwarf loves a beautiful young girl, whose seducer he murders, luring him into the costume of an ape ("Sir, it is not so much a costume as a performance") and setting him on fire; the preparation of a peasant girl for the delectation of the vile Duke Prospero (Vincent Price) and the decline of his former favourite (Hazel Court) to a sacrifice to the devil; the secret rooms, each decorated in a single colour, even to the flowers and the window glass, confinement in any one of which leads to insanity. Also made in England, *The Tomb of Ligeia* (1964) shares the same lush colour and the theatrical mood of old tombs and a ruined priory, the effete air of which Vincent Price in top hat and antique dark glasses gleefully plays up to. Among the American Poe films, though regular appearances of familiar sets and process shots destroy concentration, the energy is greater than that of the more elegant English productions. *The Fall of the House of Usher* (1960), Price obsessed by a sister whose "tainted blood" leads to his death and the house's subsidence into the mire; *The Pit and the Pendulum* (1961), where Price's revenge on an unfaithful wife and her lover produced one of art director Daniel Haller's most impressive creations, a Leonardo contraption of clanking gears and scythe-like blade beneath which the victims are strapped; *The Premature Burial* (1961), Ray Milland, in an appropriate Poe setting of Civil War America, protecting himself with pre-Victorian gadgets from the prospect of being buried alive, then being lured by his own fears into the fate he subconsciously desires — all these films shown Corman intrigued less by the horror film than by states of mind for which the stories are arresting but largely irrelevant vehicles. Under the relish for violent and sadistic death, one senses a rigorous asceticism, a contempt for the brutality of mankind masking a cold self-disgust.

Increased popularity in the mid-Sixties allowed Corman to experiment with the war film (*The Secret Invasion*, 1964) and the contemporary melodrama of violence (*The Wild Angels*, 1966) and to explore the roots of racial intolerance in *The Intruder* (1962), an adaptation of a novel by his regular scenarist Charles Beaumont whose death shortly after robbed Corman of a distinguished collaborator. A calmly professional story about the activities of an anti-integration *agent provocateur* (William Shatner) in a Southern town, its shooting was impaired when Corman, working on location, was ejected, with his crew, after locals became aware of the film's theme. All these films point to mature works like *Bloody Mama*, which expose with skill the psychological and moral pressures vexing our society, but *The Trip* (1967) most effectively relates this insight to the more personal significance of Corman's horror films. Peter Fonda's switched-off director of TV commercials takes LSD in order to understand his society and the decay of his personal relationships, and confronts a nightmare where masked riders, instruments of torture, the fantasies of childhood and the trappings of film-making pierce his secure sense of self. Ostensibly a plea for an understanding of the drug culture, and competent on that level, with Bruce Dern a persuasive apologist for Acid when used with caution, *The Trip* relates to the over-riding obsession of America and its cinema throughout the Sixties with power and licence. Recognising the symptoms to which Siegel responded with a new ethic of violence, Corman suggests as his answer a retreat to self-understanding which makes personal power irrelevant. Yet who but a saint, or a man with Corman's callous acceptance of his own spiritual disquiet, could live with the turmoil he evokes so casually in *The Trip*? Xavier, *The Man with X-Ray Eyes* (1963), blinded himself rather than exist with the agony of true insight, and for Fonda at the end of *The Trip* only suicide would seem to offer true release.

# 11. I Came, I Saw, I Lost Thirty Million Dollars

A T THE heart of Hollywood's Sixties film-making, the costume epic exemplified the faults of modern studio production and the trap into which independent producers fell. Since, in a film business based on profit, only commercial considerations were valid, even the most creative producer abandoned his artistic principles in favour of completing the film on time and guaranteeing a profit. Dazzled by the executive control so long denied them, few realised that the responsibility dictated decisions for whose stupidity they had earlier castigated their employers. If the film was to succeed, it paid to employ contract actors and writers whose ability with similar material had been tested; the inevitable result, famous profiles mouthing inanities, surprised those who recalled the statements of artistic integrity made by these producers in earlier years. Only the destruction, root and branch, of this system offered any hope of a return to "pure cinema," if such a Holy Grail had ever existed, and no one man or group of men had such power. Faced with the necessity to fish or cut bait, producers of intelligence and perception (Walter Wanger, Jerry Wald, Aaron Rosenberg) discarded their ethics to battle for Hollywood's biggest prize — the runaway success of a block-buster. Epics boomed.

A venerable cinematic form sustained by a rigid mythology, the epic thrived on Cinemascope, to whose visual conventions it was ideally suited. So enormous was the outlay on sets, costumes and cast that epics were less produced than engineered, like bridges or office buildings. Sub-contracting was the life-blood of the epic industry. Second unit directors like Yakima Canutt, Andrew Marton, Cliff Lyons and Noel Howard maintained teams of stunt and spectacle technicians and, overseas, *entrepreneurs* created facilities in the sun for American producers: Dino De Laurentiis at Rome's Cinecittá, Samuel Bronston at his huge studios outside Madrid, the Zagreb studios in Yugoslavia, all of which supplied not only sets and sound stages but also landscapes of indeterminate character equally suitable for Biblical Judea or Uzbekistan in the Twelfth century, and armies of underemployed city people willing for a few dollars a day to stand *en masse* in the sun carrying spears. Lured by low costs, tax relief and freedom from restrictive union rules, American producers kept most of

151

Europe's studios busy until the late Sixties, accepting philosophically the sameness forced on them by these shop-worn locations. Few Sixties epics have even a fraction of the flair and verisimilitude of Conway's *A Tale of Two Cities* (1935) or Van Dyke's *San Francisco* (1936), but to have made *Barabbas* or *The Bible . . . in the Beginning* under Hollywood conditions would have saddled the productions with a financial burden so crushing as to make profit impossible.

Industrial pressures restricted not only the look of an epic but its subject also. As one moves further from the hazy period of the Biblical era, costumes and architecture become more complex, and costs rise. Not since the Twenties has Hollywood been able to reproduce economically the elaborate backgrounds of Napoleonic or Renaissance times, and Sixties films attempting such a feat — most notably *Mutiny on the Bounty* (Carol Reed, Lewis Milestone, 1962) — sank under the weight of their own budgets. The logical answer was to improve the quality of story and production, lifting the film out of its epic rut into the realms of serious cinema, but this fact was grasped by only a few European film-makers, led by David Lean with *Lawrence of Arabia* and *Doctor Zhivago*, Carl Foreman with *The Guns of Navarone*, and the two in collaboration with *The Bridge on the River Kwai*, which Lean directed and Foreman wrote (without credit, because of the McCarthyite blacklist). Special effects too trade on the nebulous. Any journeyman process cameraman, free of the necessity to show a Roman trireme with any degree of accuracy, could knock up a passable Battle of Actium with an economy and ease impossible in the case of a First World War dog-fight or the breaking of a dam in some Forties European city, as inept attempts at these and other spectacles showed throughout the Sixties.

Audiences accepted the shabbiness of the epic with surprising equanimity, indifferent to howlers like wrist watches on the arms of medieval knights, (*El Cid*) sound-booms embarrassingly visible below the walls of ancient Rome (*The Fall of The Roman Empire*) or stunt men revealing blue jeans under their armour (countless films). Epics, as John Gillett pointed out, were "films for people who don't go to the pictures," using spectacle to attract an audience where beauty and truth would have failed. Not merely a big film — *Zulu*, *The Blue Max* and *Becket* are big costume pictures but not epics in the true sense — the epic invites an audience to relive the lives of action and violence they imagine people of the past enjoyed. Like the Western it returns to simpler ages of courage and direct

*Epic engineering: invading army in Spain for EL CID*

conflict and, also like the Western, loses its wider appeal when it attempts to be profound, since the first notion questioned in a thoughtful action film is that of heroism. So long as conventions like the peerless courage of the hero, his total devotion to a cause, (whether Christian, Moslem or Pagan is largely irrelevant) and a climax in which he hacks his way to victory or a heroic end for the greater good of mankind were faithfully observed, an epic's artistic quality could be abysmally low without exciting even a puzzled mutter from the audience.

Recognising this, Hollywood made its epics, if nothing else, extravagent. Since only the careful spacing of spectacular sequences could keep audiences enthralled throughout the length of an entire three-hour film, religious stories, which can be made to incorporate at least one pitched battle and conclude with the Crucifixion, have a decided edge. Audiences love the great victims, and long, in Tamerlane's phrase, to "drink the sherbet of martyrdom," a fact DeMille grasped early and made the basis of a *genre* few in the Sixties were competent to carry on. George Stevens in

*The Greatest Story Ever Told* (1965) created an honest and devout biography of Christ which, despite his talent for humane and accurate portrayals, sank in excessive reverence. No Hollywood director has dared to show Christ as more than a languid neuter, least of all Nicholas Ray in his 1961 *King of Kings*, where Jeffrey Hunter endured the Crucifixion in mortified rectitude, his James Dean pout and shaven armpits earning the film's popular retitling, *I Was a Teenage Jesus:* though it is said in Ray's defence that re-recording of Hunter's dialogue emasculated the performance. Stevens, while shrewdly casting Swedish Max von Sydow in the central role to avoid a Hollywood familiar, and shooting with 70mm in the Utah desert, could not escape the story's associations, a task accomplished only by Pier Paolo Pasolini in his earthy Marxist *Il Vangelo Secondo Matteo* (*The Gospel According to St. Matthew*). Gimmickry cancelled out Stevens's undoubted sincerity: a jug of Jordan water imported to bless the start of filming, the appearance of "guest stars," including John Wayne as the centurion ludicrously proclaiming "truly this man was the son of God," have the tang of authentic DeMille, balanced only a little by second-unit cameraman Loyal Griggs's subtly photographed desert landscapes, rendered as moody cubist compositions of silver, green and midnight blue.

Anthony Mann's sensitivity to landscape made him a master of the Western, but he adapted comfortably to the epic, transferring intact his ability to let backgrounds reflect the moral of his story. *El Cid* (1961) and *The Fall of the Roman Empire* (1964), both shot for Bronston in Spain, used the epic's obsession with disaster to describe the fall of two eras. In the first, a stylish adventure sparkling with a sense of the sea, the Spanish sun and the flair of rustic chivalry, Charlton Heston's noble warrior defeats the Moors, riding out at the climax as a corpse tied to his saddle, unconquerable even in death. Mann sets his final battle by the ocean, the two elements overlapping as two cultures interpenetrate, the garish invading army prancing up the white sand and El Cid's silver armour, flaring in the misty sun, flooding the screen with a destructive light. A lively recreation of Spanish medieval life, its jousts, tournaments and complex rules of honour gives the film a pageantry that has nothing to do with historical truth. Dealing also with historical change and decay, *The Fall of the Roman Empire* concentrates on the decline of Roman power and social purpose under Commodus (played mincingly by Christopher Plummer). On the

*KING OF KINGS: Jeffrey Hunter as Christ*

155

frontiers, skin-clad invaders lie in wait for Rome's failing legions, and in the capital temples crumble, the people and their society grow tired, a mood suggested by the enormous stone hand erected as an object of veneration, an enigmatic symbol of the empire's sickness. Playing Marcus Aurelius, Alec Guinness underlines the point with sober but apt statements of stoic philosophy as snow, darkness, corruption and death exercise their fascination. *The Heroes of Telemark* (1966), with few opportunities for virtuosity in the story of Allied ski commandos raiding a Norwegian heavy-water plant, has but a fraction of the preceding films' mood, showing in its frequent explosions the childish delight in violence that motivated a later cycle of war adventures — *The Dirty Dozen, Where Eagles Dare, Kelly's Heroes.* Amid the garrotting, knifing and demolition, Mann had little opportunity to be subtle, but the raid's execution is handled with tension, to which the gloom of a snow-filled night adds a correct sense of atmosphere.

With an overseas location vital, underdeveloped temperate areas of Europe were seldom free of Hollywood visitors. Yugoslavia, with an active film industry of its own, welcomed Hollywood's hard currency. *Genghis Khan* (Henry Levin, 1965) and *The Long Ships* (Jack Cardiff, 1964) used northern Yugoslavia (the latter's Viking village set still stands near the Italian border, a mouldering tourist attraction) though only Levin exploited the country's spectacular mountain landscape. Very much in the minor key, *Genghis Khan* upholds the best traditions of the adventure film, with Omar Sharif as Temujin, the slave who becomes Genghis Khan, and the durable Stephen Boyd his aristocratic opponent Jamuga. Like Mann, Levin lets the setting tell part of his story: a windswept plateau where Temujin's bandits hide contrasts with the lush valleys in which he was a prisoner, as the use of furs and skins gives an authentically antique effect. Woody Strode, Temujin's bodyguard, discovers the kidnapping of his chief's wife (Françoise Dorléac) when her fur robe slips silkily over a waterfall into the pool where he stands immobile, waiting to spear a fish, and her rape by Jamuga, carried out in the gloom of a skin tent, is consummated on a mound of furs. Credibility fades when the nomads visit China, there to encounter Robert Morley as the Chinese emperor and James Mason his hissing chamberlain, both recalling a road company revival of "Chu Chin Chow" (it was, in Mason's words, "the sort of film an actor does to pay his alimony"), but most of *Genghis Khan* shows a sure sense of period and an atmospheric attention to detail. This, one senses, is much how the dark ages may have been.

Even more evocative of alien times and *mores*, *The War Lord* (Franklin J. Schaffner, 1965) contrasted Charlton Heston's Eleventh Century Norman baron with the ancient religious customs of his primitive subjects. Boasting a thoughtful and poetic script (John Collier, Millard Kaufman, from Leslie Stevens's "The Lovers") and top stills photographer Eliot Elisofon as colour consultant (a task he performed also for the unremarkable *Khartoum* — Basil Dearden, 1966 — creating for that film a tranquil introductory reel of Egypt and its monuments), *The War Lord* captures the mood of an alien, superstitious people whose beliefs bewitch the conqueror as he falls in love with a girl (Rosemary Forsyth) from among them, destroying both his charge and himself. Sequences of caballistic idols found among the rocks ("This place has the dimensions of heresy," Guy Stockwell mutters as he enters the swamps and fens), of sacrifices in the fog, of Heston in his tower assailed by an alien mythology, make Schaffner's film unique. Heston, a competent actor within his range, with the undeniable ability to suggest sheer physical strength, was less extended in Nicholas Ray's *55 Days at Peking* (1963) about the resistance by a multi-racial group of diplomats inside the Consular Compound of Peking to the Boxer Rebellion. Shot in Spain on a generous budget, Ray's film is entertainingly ornate, due mainly to the efforts of art directors Veniero Colasanti and John Moore, Bronston's design specialists, whose Peking, though clearly little more than an impressive façade, convinced audiences. Between bouts of bloody fighting and the romance of Heston and aristocratic Russian bad girl Ava Gardner, Ray creates a gaudy China, aided by Dame Flora Robson and Robert Helpmann as lacquered imperial menaces and David Niven as the colony's suave spokesman; Ray too has a small part as the crippled American ambassador, and gives close attention in a superb pan shot to a charming Chinese child, the unforgettably named Lynne Sue Moon.

Among thoughtful epics, few survived the necessity for an obligatory final disaster. In the top title choice of the decade, *Sodom and Gomorrah* (Robert Aldrich, 1963, with second unit by Sergio Leone) set Stanley Baker and Anouk Aimée as incestuous brother and sister in a Sodom whose narrow stone corridors conveyed a moral malodour the script could only suggest. The tone is Victorian, even to a suggestion of that era's claustrophilic architecture, but box-office demanded some unconvincing spectacle — the destruction of a dam built by the wandering band of Lot (Stewart Granger), the heavenly onslaught that burns the cities, the turning

*SODOM AND GOMORRAH: Stanley Baker and Anouk Aimée (left)*

into a pillar of salt of Lot's wife (Pier Angeli) — which detracted from competent acting in the central roles. Another De Laurentiis project, *The Bible . . . in the Beginning* (1966), was advertised as a fifteen-hour feature to be directed by nine men, including Ingmar Bergman, Robert Bresson, Visconti, Fellini and Orson Welles, each taking one book of the Bible. Welles visited the slopes of Vesuvius scouting locations for his segment, "Sodom and Gomorrah," suggesting that this section at least would be over budget, and Bresson, invited to find an Eve for his "Garden of Eden," brought back test footage of six potential stars, all of which, to De Laurentiis's horror, were Negro or Indian; appealing to the Vatican for a ruling, he was told that Eve should be white, blonde and blue-eyed. To nobody's surprise, *The Bible* came down to one normal-length feature by the always-game John Huston, a scrapbook of Old Testament incidents from the Garden of Eden by way of Noah (played by Huston himself) and the Tower

158

*Cain (Richard Harris), slays Abel (Franco Nero) from*
*THE BIBLE ... IN THE BEGINNING*

of Babel to Abraham and Isaac. Elaborate window dressing, including an adventurous score from *avant-garde* composer Toshiro Mayuzumi, could not make *The Bible* more than a curiosity, marred by moments of high farce, the most risible being God's creation of an Adam (Michael Parks) who emerges from the dust with near-camera leg chastely upraised.

In contrast to *The Bible*, Stanley Kubrick's *Spartacus* (1960) shares the preoccupation of *The War Lord* with the underlying beliefs that explain cultures and their destruction, and despite a $12 million budget only some perfunctory battle scenes justify its "epic" label. In his novel, Howard Fast had seen Spartacus, the slave revolutionary, as the affirmation of man's ability in all eras to resist dehumanisation, an issue he explores in a careful examination of Roman attitudes to these "animate tools," their slaves, but Dalton Trumbo, in his first major screenplay since being blacklisted in the

Fifties, was less confident in his assertion of socialist principles, daunted perhaps by the director's intention to emphasise Spartacus as a contradictory personality and star Kirk Douglas to air his strong Zionist principles. Kubrick's *Spartacus* has none of the novel's depth or humanity. Seen first as a brawling slave in the Roman salt mines, Spartacus graduates to gladiatorial status with easy assurance, and thence to being leader of a slave revolt. Followers attracted by his charisma unquestioningly accept his leadership, as slave girl Jean Simmons accepts his love, and even his major opponent, the bisexual general Crassus (Laurence Olivier) admires him sufficiently to adopt his wife and child after his capture and crucifixion. But Spartacus achieves nothing. His movement flounders in an orgy of torture and death for which Trumbo's hint that his protest will be heard centuries in the future seems a meagre justification. The first film to draw universal attention to Kubrick's skill as a stylist, the entertainment value of *Spartacus* balanced its *naïveté*. Contrast is made between the politely corrupt Romans, notably Peter Ustinov's deferential slave merchant and Charles Laughton as the obese, corrupt Gracchus, an authentic Roman figure, and the ragged mob whose members occasionally achieve a simple nobility; but greater attention to Roman character and custom, out of place perhaps in the conventional epic, would have given this contrast some purpose. Among the many impressive examples of technique is a scene where Woody Strode (it can be no coincidence that a Negro actor was chosen for this role), ordered to fight Spartacus in a demonstration for Olivier's visiting party, throws away his life rather than kill the man he admires; in the sequence of Strode fencing skilfully with Douglas, Kubrick uses the wide screen with complete authority, making it a success both in terms of cinema and as a symbolic statement.

A producer accepting responsibility for a $10 million block-buster was master and slave of a production machine, as Walter Wanger discovered when he obtained 20th Century-Fox's backing in 1959 for his project *Cleopatra*. Wanger's ideas about the film — and from earlier productions like *Riot In Cell Block 11* and *I Want to Live* one has no doubt of Wagner's ability to produce good ideas — were engulfed in the emphasis on commercial success to rally Fox's $60 million deficit. To Spyros Skouras of Fox, profit transcended all, and his gesture of offering to an alarmed Wanger the scenario of the company's 1917 *Cleopatra*, starring Theda Bara, which "just needed a little updating" betrays the idiocy of conventional studio thinking. For the same reason, studio boss Buddy Adler regarded casting

*Kirk Douglas leads the revolt of the gladiators in SPARTACUS*

as making a choice from among the stars under contract rather than selecting actors suitable for the role. One wonders with what emotions Wanger viewed nominations like Cary Grant, Yul Brynner and Noël Coward to play Caesar, and Marilyn Monroe, Kim Novak, Audrey Hepburn and Shirley MacLaine for the title role; but, panicked at last, he began treating the project as an industrial rather than an artistic enterprise, as his suggestion of Alfred Hitchcock to direct the film implies. Intriguing as it is to contemplate a Coward/MacLaine/Hitchcock *Cleopatra* (with James Stewart as Antony?), only a producer and an industry with numbed critical faculties could consider such preposterous propositions.

In such a climate, the choice of box-office sure-shot Elizabeth Taylor for Cleopatra seems inevitable, and with it the problems that were to plague the production for four years. As Wagner surrendered control, Fox packed the cast with inexpensive names. Peter Finch was signed for Caesar, Stephen Boyd for Anthony. Proven technician Rouben Mamoulian agreed to direct, and half a dozen writers set to work preparing a script from the mediocre Carlo Maria Franzero biography, bought by Wanger for $15,000, on which the film is ostensibly based. A bonanza for studio departments, who in the block-buster exercised a control over the film greater than any creative artist, epic subjects were handed to the design and costume teams often before writer or director had been chosen; their work then became a frenzied pursuit of Oscar nominations, achieved by creating showy settings having little relevance to the film's atmosphere or plot. As components of the studio machine, talented designers and costumers were vital to Hollywood's golden years, but their tyranny in the Sixties emasculated countless films, drowning directors and actors in a flood of irrelevant window-dressing, a fault from which *Cleopatra* suffered to the point of destruction. One sees the power of even minor technicians in the furore caused when Miss Taylor demanded, as part of her contract terms, that hairdresser Sidney Guilaroff be retained, at $1,700 a week, to style her hair. Since the film was at that time to be shot in England (it later moved to Italy and Egypt), British *coiffeurs* protested at the infringement of union rules, and Guilaroff eventually had to appear before an extraordinary general meeting of the entire British film-making union, production being delayed while this vital issue was settled.

By September, 1959, when *Cleopatra* began shooting at Pinewood, the production had run away with itself. From an estimated $1.2 million project (to have starred Joan Collins, shot on the Fox backlot in Hollywood), it rocketed from $2 million to $3 million to $5 million to $13 million. Taylor had agreed to star at $125,000 for sixteen weeks' work, extensible at the rate of $50,000 a week thereafter, plus 10% of the gross. An additional $3,000 a week living expenses was also provided. Eventually she took between $2 and $3 million out of the film, even though her own ill-health and private affairs contributed substantially to its eventual $40 million budget. Writers were hired with the same contempt for artistic values as shown in the casting. Ex-actress Ludi Claire assembled historical material to supplement Franzero's book, and from this Nigel Balchin wrote a script which was worked over in varying degrees by Marc Brandel,

Nunnally Johnson and Sidney Buchman. Lawrence Durrell, an Alexandria *habitué*, was hired for a month's work at $7,000, with options to extend at $2,500 a week, and Paddy Chayefsky mailed in a few expensive suggestions that would have required replanning the whole script. Taylor's throat infection in March 1961 forced Wanger to write off all the footage shot at Pinewood, the various scripts and even the English sets, and when the star at last reported for work in September, 1961, Mamoulian had given way to Joseph L. Mankiewicz, who (with Ranald MacDougall and Sidney Buchman, all hard-line studio professionals) had written an entirely new script, while Richard Burton and Rex Harrison became Taylor's new screen suitors. More than $5 million had been wasted even before the eventually-released version of *Cleopatra* began, with only a few scraps salvaged. Rex Harrison recalls Burton mentioning that his sandals were uncomfortable. They, like all his costumes, were made to fit Stephen Boyd, and, in a belated burst of studio penny-pinching, never altered.

Nothing emerging from this furore could be more than an anti-climax, and one contemplates with horror the degree to which it would have failed without the contribution of Mankiewicz, whose new interpretation of the story supplied what meagre serious content *Cleopatra* has. In the new script, a shrewd repetition of Shaw's characterisation in *Caesar and Cleopatra*, Caesar, a Renaissance intellectual, cultivated and cynical, sees through Cleopatra's simple political ambitions, mocks the pretensions of power and demands kingship with a weariness suggesting he knows death is near and desires to hasten it. His remark to Antony, "Have you seen the Nile? Spare yourself the journey. It is in her eyes," implies both this wish for retirement and the total understanding between himself and the queen. Weak and self-indulgent, Antony is Caesar's shadow, pursuing Cleopatra in a desire to emulate his master and victim, a task to which he is unequal. She rightly holds him in contempt, and after a brief affair by which she hopes to save her kingdom from the invading Romans, abandons him to die in Caesar's tomb.

A smaller film, both in length and scope, might have offered an agreeable exercise in the psychological interpretation of history, but *Cleopatra* engulfed all concerned with it. The plot slows to a halt for garish tableaux concocted by the costume department — the queen's entry into Rome is preceded by hordes of dancing girls expelling birds, streamers and clouds of gold dust, Cleopatra herself perched on a golden sphinx drawn by Negro slaves. (This extravagence contrasts with the Battle of Actium sequence, shot with a bathtub fleet and ludicruous special effects). Harrison takes the few acting honours. His urbane and mocking Caesar, whether patronising the garish Egyptian court (" . . . and greetings to *you*, Pothinos, Chamberlain and Chief Eunuch, a position not acquired without certain sacrifices . . .") or lecturing an eager Cleopatra on the niceties of political warfare is a continuing delight. The film's few moments of subtlety are his, notably when suffering an epileptic fit, writhing on the marble floor with vertical shadows from a screen barring his body and Cleopatra watching from the eyes of a religious image high on the wall. But *Cleopatra*'s history dramatised the extent to which critical appraisal of any film from Hollywood in the Sixties is irrelevant; with $40 million at stake, only money has a right to talk.

\* \* \*

"Who killed Hollywood? Nobody — it isn't dead." (Or so the fashionable answer goes.) "Hollywood lives on in the minds and hearts of America" — but one wonders. Hollywood films are seldom remembered for what they were, but for what audiences wished them to be. The window on a perfect existence opened only for the Saturday evening audiences of the world, not for the men who fought ulcers and each other to create them. Judy Garland was not the girl next door, Clark Gable not the strong silent hero, Rita Hayworth not the smouldering courtesan, and a realisation that this is so corrupts totally our response to their work. Even when critics praise these films, it is with a conscious suspension of disbelief, a willingness to see in them that which people of their time expected and directors and technicians coldly provided. Hollywood's classic films, the great works of the Twenties and Thirties, have for me a sting of insight and an instinctive identification that grows more powerful as I repeatedly view them, yet I suspect that, in my desire to preserve what they meant on first viewing, a traffic in emotion has been set up in which I am increasingly the giver. Praising these now remote, faded images, I praise myself.

Hence a feeling that Hollywood in the Sixties is not truly Hollywood, but a factory whose product lacks the magic of earlier decades. Perhaps some magic will accrue over the years, but once we are aware of its mechanics will the alchemy continue to work? Like the cartoon characters, we remain suspended in the air only as long as we are unaware of being so; as soon as we look down, we fall. One film-maker at least sensed what has happened in Hollywood in the Sixties. In *Model Shop* (1969) Jacques Demy shows his eternal woman, Lola (Anouk Aimée) walking cautiously along a secluded Beverley Hills street while Los Angeles lies with a dead hush below. A thread of music accompanies her, the violin theme from *Scheherezade*, a song for the eternal story-teller who fends off death with a tale. But there is nobody to listen, and at last the music fades.

# Index

*(Major references to films appear in bold type)*

168